Stories from My Life with the
Other Animals

STORIES FROM

My Life

WITH THE

Other Animals

James McConkey

DAVID R. GODINE
PUBLISHER · BOSTON

First edition published in 1993 by
David R. Godine, Publisher, Inc.
Horticultural Hall
300 Massachusetts Avenue
Boston, Massachusetts 02115

Library of Congress Cataloging-in-Publication Data

McConkey, James.
Stories from my life with the other animals / James McConkey.—1st ed.
p. cm.
1. McConkey, James—Biography. 2. Novelists, American—20th
century—Biography.
I. Title.
ISBN 0-87923-967-0 PS3563.C3435Z472 1993
813'.54—dc20 93-15060 CIP

FIRST EDITION
Printed in the United States of America

♫Acknowledgments

Chapters in this volume first appeared in the following magazines: "Contextual Surprises" and "Stories from My Life with the Other Animals" in *The Hudson Review,* "A Family Record" in *The New Yorker,* and "Heroes Among the Barbarians" in *Shenandoah.*

Grateful acknowledgment is made to Chatto & Windus (London) for permission to reprint an excerpt from "The Return to the Present," a portion of *Contre Sainte-Beuve* by Marcel Proust, translated by Sylvia Townsend Warner, translation copyright 1957 by Chatto & Windus Ltd., and published in the U.S.A. by Meridian Books, Inc. as *Marcel Proust on Art and Literature, 1896–1919* (Greenwich editions, 1958).

Contents

"All this I do inside me, in the huge court of my memory.
There I have by me the sky, the earth, the sea,
and all things in them which I have been able to perceive. . . .
There too I encounter myself. . . ."
—*St. Augustine*

Foreword

Stories from My Life with the Other Animals is the third and concluding volume of *Court of Memory,* a more than thirty-year exploration of an ever-expanding personal past. When I embarked upon this autobiographical journey in 1960, I had no idea that it would go very far. It began out of personal need—from a desire that came to me late on a winter night, as nuclear war seemed an imminent possibility, to acknowledge my love for my family and the sacredness I felt in everything about me, and to communicate my truths, however subjective they might be, to anybody who would listen. The period covered by the three volumes approximates that of the Cold War. Though humanity faces problems of such urgency that they must be solved if we are to endure through the next millenium, the Cold War, at least, has become history. The reasons I am ending my account are only tangentially related to the ending of the Cold War, but I suppose *Stories from My Life with the Other Animals* and the two volumes that precede it can be read as the story of an American—a representative one, I hope—who was led to consider the possible meanings and the value of his life against the threat of mass extinction in the epoch that fortunately has come to a close.

My first autobiographical narrative was called "A Night Stand," and it appeared in *Perspective,* a now defunct literary magazine edited by Jarvis Thurston of Washington University in St. Louis. Since its circulation was limited, I was surprised and gratified that seven of the readers of its winter 1960 issue wrote me to say that my contribution reflected some of their own feelings. I suppose it is because of those seven letters and postcards that I wrote a second account, and then a third. Though in recent years other writers have begun what appear to be continuing autobiographies (and some have led more remarkable lives than I), I've not come across one quite like *Court of Memory,* in which each chapter works from a given event in the present, reaching back through memory for analogies that will give resonance and at least a transitory sense of completion or synthesis to it. In work of this sort, the changing as well as the constant aspects of self can be defined at any number of fixed moments along the curve of personal time. Each of the events that mark these fixed moments generates, through the workings of memory, a separate story or essay, while also serving as part of a larger narrative. With its repetitions, variations, and additions, such a structure approximates the rhythmic process of living, at least as I have experienced it. I owe that structure not to any predetermined plan, but to memory itself, as well as the seven readers of *Perspective* who got me started on it.

The first volume was published in 1968 under the title *Cross-*

roads: An Autobiographical Novel. That title was supplied by the publishing firm, whose editors, puzzled by what seemed to them a new form, wanted to see the book as a combination of two traditional genres. (The title I had proposed, *Seven Years in the Life of an Amateur Astronomer,* struck them, properly enough, as misleading; they were encouraged to think of it as an "autobiographical novel" by my own, and still continuing, tendency to refer to each of its parts as "story" and "narrative" as well as "essay.") But the inclusion of "novel" in the title, which led some early readers to wonder if the events, or at least some of them, were invented, was unfortunate; for to have invented *any* event or person would have been a violation of my most crucial rule for this kind of writing. That first volume centers largely on my family, particularly on my relationships with my wife and our growing children. *Court of Memory,* as it was published in 1983, adds a second volume, "The Stranger at the Crossroads," to the first. Since our children were no longer the center of family life, the fixed moments in this volume are concerned with strangers, casual acquaintances, neighbors, and old friends—and sometimes with death. (When a copy of the dust jacket for the 1983 edition was sent to me for approval, I was disconcerted to find that the phrase "An autobiographical novel"—at the bottom and in small print—had reappeared. At my request, these words were deleted, the artist replacing them with a green feather.)

While this concluding volume of *Court of Memory* refers back to events narrated in the earlier two, it has its own concerns; they are shared, I imagine, by others of my age. Animals—and to a lesser degree, music—figure prominently in these accounts. They tend to be longer than the earlier ones. The growing length of the rhythms of thought and feeling in our later years may

come from an unconscious desire to sum things up—a desire
I recognized as mine only while writing the last chapter in this
last volume.

* * *

I've never satisfactorily resolved one problem inherent in the
form that memory has given me. It concerns naming—the identification of others, some of whom are intimately connected with
my life. From the beginning, I felt a need to protect others from
my often subjective intrusions into their private lives. In the
opening sections of *Crossroads*, I avoided even the names of
family members, making my references to them sound almost
like generic titles—"my wife," for example, or "my older son" for
members of my immediate family; and "my father," "my mother,"
"my brother," "my aunt," and "my cousin" for the larger family
group. (A feminist once told me that every time she tried to read
Crossroads, she ended up throwing it against the wall. When I
asked her the cause of her anger, she said, "Every time you
mention your wife, you call her *your wife*.") Gradually, I gained
sufficient confidence in my ability to avoid harm to my children
(at least, in my prose!) to call them by their given names. My
wife's middle name is Jean, and is my intimate name for her as
well as the one that recalls her presence in periods of absence;
but since it is not her public name, it has provided me enough
of a psychological screen, or necessary aesthetic distance, to
make the person closest to me something other than "my wife."

During the writing of *Court of Memory*, all the members of
the family I was born into have died, and so have many of the
friends, colleagues, acquaintances, and other relatives who figure
in it. Since I never asked permission for writing about these
people, I have often used pseudonyms or some other subterfuge;

now that I have reached the end, I regret that I have not been able to honor them directly. Had I remembered my past from a single fixed point of my seventy-first year, I probably could have used their actual names; but I would have written, of course, an entirely different book.

—JAMES MCCONKEY

1993

1984

⮑Younger Voices, Earlier Rooms

M Y W I F E , Jean, became pregnant with our first child, Larry, during our second year as graduate students— she in biochemistry, I in English—at the University of Iowa. As a recently discharged veteran of the Second World War, I was attending school on the GI bill and had a part-time teaching job; while completing the research for her thesis—the topic was "Some Laboratory Tests for the Study of Liver and Biliary Tract Disease"—Jean worked in the University of Iowa hospital laboratory of her thesis director, where, among other tasks unconnected with her research, she analyzed blood samples of motorists charged with driving while intoxicated. Frequently she traveled to one courthouse or another in the eastern half of the state to testify in the trials of those involved in accidents whose blood samples she had found to contain alcohol in excess of the legal limit for drivers.

Our child was expected toward the end of September; in Iowa, the late summer months tend to be exceptionally hot and humid, marvelous for corn but uncomfortable for a woman nearing the end of her pregnancy. Jean and I were accustomed to work together—both of us, for example, had dug the four-foot-deep trench for the water line to the small trailer we bought and put on concrete blocks in a field after a fruitless search for an apartment upon our arrival in Iowa City, and we studied together in that cozy home—but now she, of course, carried the growing child within herself. She continued her testimony at court trials and her general work in the hospital lab, although by early September she had to stand sideways to the bench with its flasks and Bunsen burners. She felt it entirely reasonable to stay at her job until the birth was imminent; when the contractions became severe, she said, all she would need to do, if she were at work, was to walk down some steps to the labor room. Besides, she added, the lab, while devoid of air conditioning, was convenient to a machine in the corridor that produced shaved ice at the touch of a button, and she craved shaved ice all day long.

That summer I taught no classes, and should have been studying for my literary history examination, a two-day written part followed by a four-hour oral in which specialists in every field of English and American literature probed for lacunae in the candidate's knowledge; but I was restless and desired to be more creative than that—and so, within one of the two cubicles of that twenty-five-foot trailer whose roof shimmered in the heat of the Iowa sun, I tried to write a story. My arm kept sticking to the desk top, much as it had when I had been forced to practice the Palmer method of penmanship—use the *arm*, not the wrist—in an equally suffocating Little Rock schoolroom in June.

"Jimmy, you're cheating again," my fourth-grade teacher would say severely, having once more surprised me from behind as I wiggled the pen with my wrist; an effective spy, she always wore crepe-soled shoes. It seemed to me that I was cheating now, too; day after day, my efforts were abortive.

In our forty years of marriage, Jean and I have rarely quarreled—and the majority of our spats came during a few months of that first pregnancy. She seemed to me so sensible and self-contained, so impervious, that I felt unwanted, jealous—an old fault, from my childhood. During the long summer evenings, I compounded my loneliness by taking walks by myself and missing the deceased Houlihan, a cocker spaniel we had bought the previous year and whose name had come from the major character of my first (and only) published story. I had been paid three hundred dollars for it, a handsome sum for a piece of fiction written quickly, with excitement and pleasure—or so it now seemed to me, trudging along a country road near the Iowa City airport—in the first weeks of our life in a trailer that then hadn't seemed confining in the slightest.

Jean and I had celebrated the acceptance of that story with a dinner at the downtown hotel, where we decided to use some of the money to buy a puppy. After she returned from work one lovely October afternoon, we ate an early supper and then drove to an Amana colony about thirty miles away in response to a classified advertisement offering cocker spaniels for sale. Tumbling over each other in a backyard pen, the puppies were barely distinguishable from each other; since we couldn't decide which one to choose, the owners, a middle-aged couple of the communal sect—the wife wearing a long gown and bonnet, the husband a black suit, for they had been ready to leave for evening religious services when we arrived—invited us into their parlor, placed the puppies on a white sheet in the middle of the bare floor, and told us they would return in an hour and a half. As in a Shaker dwelling, ladderback chairs hung from pegs on the walls; we lay on the sheet with the puppies, letting them climb over us and lick our faces as dusk came, bringing with it—seemingly just beyond the many-paned window—the harvest moon.

O, Houlihan, dog named for the first successful offspring of my imagination, warm-bodied and floppy-eared little creature who, exhausted by paroxysms of love, fell asleep on my neck in a moon-drenched setting more enchanting in its austerity than any I ever devised with plump adjectives!—I built for you a fenced run and small pitched-roof house, so you could have both fresh air and shelter while I was away at my classes; I bought you cans of nourishing food and aroused your finicky appetite by lying next to your bowl and growling as if I wanted the soupy chunks for myself; I taught you to skid on your rump even while chasing a ball whenever you neared the curb, that frontier of grim no-dog's-land where puppies become pancakes; but I could not overcome the attraction to water that made you jump into every creek and pond on our walks together nor stay the spread of the pneumococci that ravaged your lungs following your final, cold swim.

Poor Houlihan was but a pawn, like a child's doll, enabling Jean as well as me to rehearse parenthood for the human life to come; doubtlessly our grief at his passing—the veterinarian said he was a victim of inbreeding—made us realize how much he had served as a surrogate for a child. And yet, now that life stirred within her, I felt myself another such a pawn. Perceiving that a baby in that trailer would intensify the claustrophobia that both of us had come to find within it, Jean managed to get an advance list of the summer graduates at the university, and made calls until she found a departing graduate student couple who had not yet promised their apartment to another.

This apartment, which we immediately rented, was on the third floor of what once had been an imposing single-family residence; the doors to all the rooms of the first and second floor apartments opened off the halls surrounding the central stair-case. As attic dwellers, we had a hallway for our use only; sepa-rated from the stairwell by a railing, it connected the small bath at the head of the stairs to the rest of the apartment. That hallway widened into a kind of vestibule between our two rooms—one a kitchen and the other a living room with a window alcove large enough for a bed. We decided to use the vestibule as a nursery; my thought (later I was to discover I had the problem in reverse) was to construct a wall to protect our sleeping infant from the domestic noises coming up the stairwell from the first two floors, for the families beneath us kept all their doors open, particularly in warm weather, and the clatter of pans, the laughter and the arguments, as well as the screams of small children, wafted upward with the hot air. The landlord, though, forebade me from driving a single nail into the plaster. I still couldn't write or concentrate on my studies, but my success in building Houli-han's doghouse gave me a faith in my skill at carpentry to which the landlord's interdiction only provided a challenge: I designed and constructed a self-standing wall—a combination cabinet (deep enough for diapers and other nursery supplies) and book-case reaching from floor to ceiling, sturdy enough to support a door frame bearing the weight of the heavy second-hand door I hinged to it. The landlord liked my workmanship enough to take off half-a-month's rent; to show that the wall was now part of the house and belonged to him, he papered the back with the same paper that decorated the stairwell. That self-standing wall was my major achievement in the months of Jean's pregnancy.

*   *   *

A few evenings after she testified in a trial in a distant town (because of the nearness of the birth, I went along), Jean didn't return from work. I called the laboratory, but received no answer; only moments later, a nurse phoned to tell me that my wife had asked her to let me know she was in the labor room. I said I would be right there; the nurse replied that I would not be permitted to see her, and should stay where I was, since the baby probably wouldn't be born that night. "We'll call you as soon as your wife goes to the delivery room," the nurse said. "That's a promise. Relax. You know what's good for expectant fathers?" "What?" I asked. "Solitaire," she said. "See if you can win at solitaire."

Since I could neither eat nor follow the lines in a book, I made a pot of coffee and obediently put a deck of cards on the kitchen table. At first I hesitated to play solitaire. What if I didn't win? Would that mean trouble for Jean and the baby? What if, though, having been advised to play, I refused? Might that not bring an even greater disaster? I am now sixty-two and have three grown sons, but I remain as superstitious as ever. Like a character in Shakespeare, I find portents in comets, meteorites, and the pulsating curtains of auroral displays. I have long since refused to pick up those milky pebbles that children call lucky stones, for I have forgotten which shoulder one is supposed to throw them over and I've found general disagreement on the matter—although everybody agrees that bad luck comes if you choose the wrong shoulder.

On that night before Larry's birth, I finally decided that I *should* play a hand of solitaire. I won, which meant that neither my wife or child was to be punished for my meanness of spirit during the pregnancy. But did it really mean that? Maybe to win a single game was mere chance. I played a second hand, winning just as readily. Should I attempt a third hand? To pit all the luck I'd won on a third game—that was like winning or losing a fortune at Monte Carlo or Las Vegas, except that here the turn of the cards involved a fortune in human lives. Alarming my heart, which wanted to escape from the rest of me, I gambled everything—and won again. Over the years, Jean and I have played solitaire—usually before a Coleman lantern at a remote campsite during one of our canoe trips in the Adirondacks—but never since that night have I won three times in a row. Having done so, I climbed into the alcove bed, patted the unoccupied pillow, and fell into such a deep and serene slumber that, if the telephone did ring just before Larry was born at 2 A.M., I didn't hear it.

I found Jean in her maternity ward bed in the morning, nursing a snub-nosed and fuzzy-haired baby with delicate fingernails and all those other miraculous attributes like eyelids and lashes and knuckles that in adults are beneath notice. "I'm sorry I wasn't here," I said, out of breath from jumping the stairs two at a time. She said, "Neither was the doctor. The birth—and isn't he lovely?—caught everybody by surprise, he came so quickly. It was the easiest and most natural thing in the world."

"I knew it would be like that," I said.

"How did you know?"

"I just did, that's all. And I know both of you will have long and fortunate lives."

"We will, if you do," Jean said.

"I've always had good luck," I said huskily, rubbing my eyes before kissing her on the cheek. "That's because I'm such a whiz-bang at solitaire."

"There's just one tiny problem, maybe, with the baby," Jean said.

If expectant fathers are emotional, lost to petty jealousies, new fathers leap at an instant from happiness to hysteria. "My God, what do you mean?" I asked.

"Well, he *cries.*"

"Don't all babies? They're different from puppies."

"The nurse who brought him to me just now says there's always one baby in the ward who cries more loudly than the others."

"So ours has the loudest cry?" I was proud of that.

"She says ours has the strongest lungs she's ever heard."

"That's a good sign. That means he has sounder lungs than Houlihan. He's obviously the healthiest child in the world. Look how blissful he is now." For Larry had fallen asleep at her breast.

Jean and the baby came home two days later, much sooner than was customary in those years, but her doctor felt both of them to be in unusually fine shape. Since Jean had been working in the hospital, his services came under the category of "professional courtesy"; and the doctor gave Jean the telephone number of the pediatrics clinic, the services of which were also free, and which could be contacted day or night in case of an emergency. At first, we kept the crib at the foot of our bed, so that we could respond immediately to any problem that Larry might have. He slept peacefully, but it seemed as though one or the other of us was always awake, listening to him breathe. How extraordinary a new life is! But what anxiety it brings! Should he be awakened for a feeding or not? For two weeks we worried simply because he slept so soundly.

*   *   *

Although thirty-five years have passed since his birth, I am often reminded at noon of Larry's cries from the third week onward, for the daily test of the siren on top of the firehouse in the hamlet of Mecklenburg three miles from our home in the Finger Lakes countryside is similar to my memory of that sound. The test begins softly—a low, even a tender, murmur—and then rapidly rises in pitch and intensity until, exhausted by its upward wail, it fades into silence. The siren, though, is controlled by a timer, and ceases after a single warning scream. Every muscle in Larry's body became tense, causing his back to arch and his legs to stiffen, as if he were ready to undergo a convulsion during each of his crescendos. His muscles would relax for a moment as he prepared all of his tiny resources for the next mighty wail. On the first night he cried like that, Jean and I took turns holding him, which only seemed to worsen his anguish. At last I went off to the bathroom for a rest, taking along as justification—for classes had commenced—the Old Norse text for the graduate seminar in which I was a student and a book of poems for the course I taught.

The bathroom was separated from the rest of the apartment by the wall I had built—a wall that, as I discovered at once, was no barrier to the power of my son's lungs. Looking down the stairwell, I saw that lights were on in both apartments beneath ours; I heard toilets flushing, a child calling her mother. On the floor directly below a man wearing nothing but Jockey shorts stumbled down the hallway and then back, as if he had forgotten his drowsy destination. Slinking against the wall, I tiptoed to the bathroom, where I ignored both of my texts for every item in a full-page A & P ad in the newspaper I found draped over the rim of the tub. As I was returning to give Jean her turn at freedom, the cries stopped. Jean motioned me into the kitchen, shutting the door behind us; for Larry was asleep in the crib by our bed. I asked her in relief, "What did you do?"

"I called the emergency number."

"What did the doctor say?"

"Something about an underdeveloped nervous system."

"An *underdeveloped nervous system?*"

"Shhh. It's normal—you wouldn't expect an infant to be completely developed in every respect, would you? An underdeveloped nervous system can cause a mild colic. If a baby has an unusually loud cry, the parents understandably become nervous themselves. They transfer their own tension to the infant, which intensifies his colic. It's a vicious circle."

"You're just repeating, word for word, what he told you." For Jean was as calm and reasonable as she had been during the pregnancy, and I felt that she was treating me as if I were the baby.

"Didn't you ask me to tell you what the doctor said? I'm trying to stay relaxed, as he told me both of us should be."

"So you relaxed and Larry immediately fell asleep?"

"No, I put him back in the crib to cry himself out. If his colic returns, we'll just have to let him cry, at least for tonight."

"And tomorrow?"

"Tomorrow, before you come home, you're to go to the drugstore to buy a baby's hot water bottle, the kind with a hose for enemas."

"We're supposed to give him an *enema?*"

She looked at me thoughtfully, calculating—as I realized the following night—what, given my resources, I should hear. "That's simply so you'll know the kind to buy, silly. It's to warm his stomach."

Larry slept for the rest of the night, and was still sleeping when I left for class. I returned in the early afternoon with the hot water bottle to find Jean holding a well-rested and happy baby; though she had shadows beneath her eyes, she was as tranquil and radiant as a Renaissance Madonna. "I don't think we'll need that," she said, with a glance at my purchase. "He's so sweet-tempered, such a joy! I'd say he smiled at me this morning if the woman on the first floor hadn't told me a smile in a baby so young is a sure sign of colic."

To indicate our confidence in ourselves, and to communicate to Larry the casualness of our relationship with him, we put his crib where it belonged, in the hallway nursery. All three of us fell asleep soon after dusk. Jean rose once, to feed him, on schedule. Half an hour later, just as we were drowsing off, we heard what we now recognized as the soft prelude to the most piercing of cries. "Are you relaxed?" I whispered to her. "Oh, absolutely," she said, and both of us laughed. She said, "I imagine he needs another diaper."

A dry diaper did stop his crying. He seemed comfortable enough, even though he wouldn't sleep and his stomach made odd sounds. We obviously had assumed the proper attitude; but, to make sure Larry remained content, we decided to warm his stomach with the rubber bottle. While Jean filled the bottle, I held Larry on my lap in our new rocker, and something about the glide of the chair and the softness of his blanket gave me the melody and some of the words to a song I wasn't aware that I knew. The words seemed, in my memory, to be coming from my mother's young voice. " 'Lazy John,' " I said, astonished.

[13]

"What did you say?" Jean asked, testing the warmth of the bottle before gently placing it between the blanket and the flannel of Larry's sleepers.

"The most remarkable thing just happened," I said in excitement. "Something clicked in my mind, making verbal sense out of a feeling from before I knew words, from the time I was a baby like Larry."

"Stay calm," Jean said.

"My mother rocked me and sang me to sleep with 'Lazy John.' It goes like this," and, vigorously rocking, I sang,

Lazy John, when the sun is shining,
Slowly turns from the light away,

before asking Jean, "Do you know what that means?"

"What it says," she said. "Hold the water bottle on his stomach."

"It means that nearly from birth every experience is imprinted on the mind. Every moment is crucial to a baby's development. It means that this very moment will be deep within Larry's memory—"

"He's starting to tense up," Jean said tensely.

Entranced by the mysteries of memory, I began to sing again,

Lazy John, when the sun is shining,
Slowly turns from the light away,

pausing only long enough to say in triumph, "I've got it, Jean! I've got the whole stanza!" before completing the verse:

Only murmuring, "How surprising,
People wake at the break of day."

My last words, though, were swept away in the enormity of that now familiar wail.

The three of us, and no doubt all the occupants of the house, were awake until nearly dawn. I don't like to think that "Lazy John," which gave me nothing but security as a baby, had much to do with Larry's distress; after all, his stomach had been grumbling beforehand. (Whatever my theory about imprinting, that song couldn't have made an impression on Larry one way or another, for during a recent long distance telephone call, I asked him if he remembered "Lazy John," and he asked, "Who's he?") We couldn't get him to cry himself to sleep in his crib, even with the hot water bottle; indeed, he screamed with such vigor that he turned blue. "I thought he was beginning to turn blue last night," Jean said, picking him up. It's difficult to stay calm while your baby is screaming himself blue, but Jean managed it better than I. She told me to fetch the Vaseline, some baby soap, and a pan. "Put some warm water in the pan, and swish the soap around in it," she directed, rocking Larry. After I completed that task, she said, "Now put some Vaseline on the tip of the hose."

"My God," I cried, my voice nearly as shrill as our baby's. "You don't expect me to—"

"There's no risk if only we can stay calm," Jean said. "The doctor said it was our last resort."

Although we took turns holding Larry in various peculiar positions as the other timidly tried to insert the slippery tip in his rectum, we managed only to drench him and ourselves with the soapy water, while causing his little buttocks to become even bluer than his face had been the last time we saw it. Jean wiped suds from her eye. "Do you suppose he's up to a bath?" she asked nervously. "He certainly needs one."

Actually, it was the warm bath water that worked the miracle, causing his muscles to relax. He fell asleep as Jean was sloshing water on his belly, and we smiled wanly at each other. "Now we know what to do," she said, but I thought we ought to take him back to the hospital. "Something's got to be wrong," I said. "Babies aren't supposed to turn blue, are they?"

And so, sneaking out of the house in the morning while the other occupants overslept their jobs and classes, we drove Larry to the clinic. "What's the trouble?" a young intern asked heartily, as we were ushered into his examination room. I said our baby cried until he turned blue.

"Is this your first child?" the intern asked.

"Yes," Jean said.

"I see," the intern said, taking a docile Larry in his arms. He weighed the baby, looked into his ears and eyes, flexed his joints, and so on. It was the cold stethoscope on his chest that produced the first tightening of Larry's muscles, the initial cry. The sound surprised the intern, and he looked at us for reassurance. "That's how he cries," I said. The intern gave Larry's face, stomach, and legs a professional scrutiny. "By golly, he does turn blue all over, doesn't he? Hold on to him, I'll be right back." And he rushed out of the room to return almost at once with three older doctors and a nurse. The intern said, "You see, he does turn blue." Listening to Larry's continuing screams, one of the older doctors said, "No wonder," and asked Jean how she managed to quiet him. She said that a warm bath that morning had finally put him to sleep. The newcomers repeated as much of the examination as Larry would permit.

As Jean was trying both to comfort and bundle up our child, a white-haired doctor wrote out a prescription, handing me the slip. "How often should we give him the medicine?" I asked, trying unsuccessfully to read the scribbles. "My dear boy, the sedative is for you and your wife," he said, patting my shoulder. "As for your baby, just continue with the warm baths."

*   *   *

Gradually, Larry's nervous system developed; in a couple of months, it caught up with his lungs, the two working as a coordinated team to signal, to the neighborhood, various kinds of distress that Jean, after decoding the specific cry, usually could alleviate before he changed color. That is to say, he was manageable—barely—as long as she could keep him to his normal schedule; if, however, some disturbance woke him at the wrong time, he required a warm bath and much patient rocking.

Upon our arrival in Iowa City, we had been told ours was the two-hundred-and-forty-third name on the university's waiting list for married students' housing; the birth of our son, however, allowed us to leapfrog over childless couples, and our length of stay gave us priority for one of the apartments hastily put together from war-surplus barracks as part of the school's continuing attempt to catch up with the burgeoning needs of veterans and their families. Thinking chiefly of the welfare of the other tenants of our house, Jean and I decided to move; they—fathers, mothers, children—gladly helped us carry our possessions down two flights of stairs to the car.

That decision to move is an example of how error can occur if the guilty flush of solicitude is permitted to overwhelm judgment. Our new apartment was half of a barracks, separated from the adjoining apartment by a Beaverboard wall much flimsier than the one I had built. Half of a barracks is half of a long and narrow space, and is suitable for soldiers, especially when asleep. Our space had been partially domesticated by a partition, also of

Beaverboard, maybe ten feet in length and five feet high, movable at the tenants' whim or in accordance with the number of infants it was intended to sequester; and by a kitchen unit that resembled a metal wardrobe and contained a miniaturized sink, oven, and refrigerator topped by gas burners. Whenever the oven was heated, its sides expanded, causing the rack to fall. An alarm clock woke all three of us very early on our first morning, and Jean and I accused each other of setting it—until we realized that it was ringing in the adjoining apartment. In the evenings, while Larry slept, we kept the radio at low volume, tuned to a station that played classical music, and even though we gradually increased the volume as we heard a distant clanking—the sign that steam was rushing toward us through the pipes of that village of barracks— Brahms and Mozart and Tchaikovsky were normally inadequate to prevent Larry from waking to add his voice to the triumphant hammer blows announcing the arrival of heat to our radiators, at the end of the line.

Once we were unwise enough to invite a bachelor about five years older than I to dinner; he was an instructor in my department. At the table, we told him of the problems of barracks living, and he suggested that we do what he and his roommate had done. They had walked the streets of Iowa City, looking for the house they would most like to inhabit. Finding it—a many-roomed Victorian structure set in estate-like grounds—they knocked at the door and so charmed the two occupants, a widow and her spinster sister, that not only were they granted an immense bedroom with its own fireplace, but the run of the house and even the use of an elderly limousine. The house was so solidly constructed that the roommate, a baritone with hopes of a career in opera, could practice in the music room at any hour of the night without bothering anybody. Young parents with limited resources can listen with inexhaustible curiosity to descriptions of houses like that, and Jean and I asked him question after question. He said, expansively, that we might be able to live there, too—especially since he was thinking of moving to another address.

"Why would you ever leave?" Jean asked.

He said the two sisters prepared breakfast for him and his friend each morning, but that the widow, despite his protestations, always separated the segments of his grapefruit with a knife. Since she couldn't see very well, a bit of skin was attached to each segment.

Jean and I looked at each other in astonishment. The distant clanking of pipes began. "Be prepared," Jean said. The bachelor smiled politely; but I noticed that a tic developed in one of his eyes as the hammer blows were followed by the wail, and in the following months he never again mentioned the possibility of our living in that grand house, either with or without him.

To later and more enlightened generations, a further and more critical error that Jean and I made must seem quaint or beyond comprehension. She had quit her job on the day Larry was born; but, whatever the baby's demands, she managed to complete her master's thesis at home. Her committee admired her work, and suggested she use it as the basis of a dissertation which, if accompanied by an additional year of graduate study, would provide her with a doctorate. Although I had nearly exhausted my GI benefits, Jean and I might have found part-time jobs and taken turns caring for the baby so that both of us eventually would have gained the same degree. It simply didn't occur to me to make such a sacrifice; I thought of myself as the one responsible for my family's welfare, and both of us assumed my career would take precedence over hers.

So, while Jean cared for Larry in that dark barracks with its small, ceiling-high windows—years later, she told me she would stand on a chair just to be able to gaze out at another, larger world—I was away from home except for meals and sleeping; after supper, I always returned to my university office, studying well past midnight in the attempt to make up for my lack of proper effort the previous summer. Late at night, another candidate would join me, so that we could ask ourselves the hardest of the questions we expected, during our respective orals; agonizing over his answers, my compatriot would rip his fingernails into the plaster of the wall. Daily, the janitor would sweep up the powder and flakes; once he warned me the debris probably was caused by weakening beams in the old structure, which meant that the building itself might collapse in the next strong wind. Of the ten candidates who took the examination, the one with the torn fingernails and I were the only ones to pass, and he was hospitalized immediately with a bleeding ulcer. The reason that I survived the examination relatively undamaged (it did take me several years before I was capable of dreaming up a story again) was that I always recognized how lucky I was to have an office far removed from my son's cries; had Larry been a more tractable infant, I might neither have studied so diligently nor discovered so much genuine late-night pleasure in recondite literary matters.

＊　＊　＊

That summer I found a position as a teacher at a small college in an eastern Kentucky hollow, where Larry's appallingly robust cries were transformed into a vitality of body and mind that has given him an engaging optimism and a ready dexterity ever since his second year; before he was three he was adept enough with a hammer to nail together the pieces of wood I had sawed for a kitchen cabinet, and soon was surreptitiously mastering the neighboring boy's bicycle we said he was too young for and demanding piano lessons. Indeed, we were so happy to have him that we decided on another baby, who fortunately didn't cry much, and still another, who did. By then we had moved to upstate New York; instead of sleeping pills for the parents, our Ithaca pediatrician prescribed a non-narcotic liquid for that third infant, a nippleful of which, given ten minutes before a feeding, quelled his colicky protests.

Jean and I have lived for nearly a quarter century in a Greek Revival farmhouse that antedates by at least fifty years the Victorian mansion which the bachelor so tantalized us with, a farmhouse nearly as large and as sturdily constructed. It may not have an estatelike setting, but it does have an acre or so of grassy backyard in which dandelions, buttercups, daisies, and chicory bloom in their respective seasons; at the far edge of the yard, beyond the now unused softball backstop, are scattered the unmarked graves of any number of beloved small animals that one by one replaced Houlihan, the catalyst of my desire for fatherhood. Here our children all arrived at maturity, one son for each of the three games of solitaire whose winning gave me such elation on the night Jean was in labor with our first; the younger two, Cris and Jimmy, live with us while studying, after lengthy periods of absence, for their own college degrees and proposed vocations. Larry and his wife live in Manhattan, where they follow contiguous professional careers, much as my wife and I do in Ithaca. Long ago, Jean fashioned for herself, out of two of her major interests, a career as editor and writer for scientific publications.

Our house is on a high plateau, exposed to wind and the

eternality of sun and sky; it is the solitary dwelling at a country crossroads whose empty roads in starlight are but ghostly pointers to the four directions of Earth and to the sections of the dome above. On those frequent days of the present July in which I am by myself (for Cris and my namesake are taking summer courses to make up for lost time, and leave for Cornell each morning with Jean), the house is so quiet that from my open study window I can hear the whisper of the heavily bearded wheat in the field across the road. At my age, I like hours of silence in a large house beneath a vast sky, so long as I know they will end with the arrival of ones I love; I have no sentimental wish to return either to the Iowa trailer in which Jean and I initiated our long journey through parenthood or to the unsatisfactory, scream-filled rooms from which as a young husband I fled.

Earlier this month, after a couple of days of searching, Cris, Jimmy, Jean, and I found the body of Ben, our old Irish setter, in the corner of the woods he apparently had selected for his peaceful dying. At first it seemed to me a rebuke that he, unlike our other pets, had removed himself from us at such a critical moment; but then I thought that he—as a dog whose ancestors had been bred for hunting—probably carried in his genes a desire for the solitude of his favorite woods at a time like that. We decided to bury him in the location he had chosen, even though it was difficult to dig around the rocks and through the tangle of buried roots. It was an untypical evening, as hot and humid as one in Iowa, although the woods were infested with the fierce mosquitoes and black flies customary to upstate New York during any damp July. I took a turn with the pickaxe out of obligation to Ben, but soon found myself sweating and gasping for breath, and so was glad to relinquish the work to my sons. While fatherhood knows a brief and perhaps illusory period of guardianship and control, it is preceded by a helplessness that arrives months in advance of the first cries, and is followed by an ever-increasing inability to match the prowess of much more than an offspring's lungs, a fact that a parent might as well gracefully accept.

For a burial sheet, Jean had brought a section of a worn chenille bedspread on which was embroidered a cowboy on horseback, a lasso in his hand; it had belonged to each of our children in turn. Except for one paw and the tip of a once splendid plumed tail, the bedspread concealed Ben's body as Cris and Jimmy dug a grave far deeper than I had imagined possible in ground so much more resistant than the black loam of Iowa. Looking at that shroud while our sons completed the digging, Jean and I alike reached for the other's hand. Later, as we lay in bed, she and I decided that, before the summer was over, we'd go searching together for a floppy-eared puppy—which shows, I guess, that we've returned in spirit to our family's quiet beginnings.

1985

A

Family
Record

ONE DAY this past summer, I received a phone call from a staff member of the Division of Unclaimed Funds of the Ohio Department of Commerce in Columbus, who had managed to trace me to my Finger Lakes farmhouse, ten miles from Ithaca, New York; he wanted to know if I was the only survivor of my childhood family. I said yes—that my father, Clayton; my mother, Grace; and my older brother and only sibling, Jack, had all died. He said that eighteen hundred dollars remained in an Olmsted Falls, Ohio, bank account in the name of Grace McConkey and her son Jack, and that he required some verification that Jack as well as Grace was dead, and proof that I was indeed the younger son. I surprised myself by being able to recall for him the dates of the deaths of my parents and brother, as well as their ages. I told him that my father had died in 1972 in Olmsted Falls on his seventy-seventh birthday, November 24th—which also, though I didn't tell him this, was the date of my parents' first marriage, in 1915, and of their remarriage, in 1938, a ceremony at which I was the only witness; that my brother had died, at fifty-six, on July 15, 1974, in a car accident at the entrance to O'Hare Airport, near Chicago; and that my mother, who in her final decade had lived with my wife and me and two of our sons, had died on December 13, 1982, a few weeks after her grandchildren and great-grandchildren—the latter all on my brother's side—had joined my family at our farmhouse for a celebration of her hundredth birthday. On the day that my mother left Olmsted Falls to live with us, she withdrew the funds from her major account there to transfer them to another in an Ithaca bank; apparently, I said, she had forgotten about the other account, which I assumed had been set up for the monthly sums my brother and I had sent to our parents as a supplement to their Social Security checks. The caller asked me to forward to his office whatever evidence I had that I was indeed Grace's only surviving child—including, if I could find any of her correspondence, a letter containing her Olmsted Falls address. I told him I would try. But for some weeks I put it off, not wanting, especially for something so grubby as cash, to burrow into the boxes in the closet of my mother's former bedroom, which was where my wife, Jean, knowing I wasn't up to sorting through them in the Christmas season following my mother's death, had put all of Grace's possessions.

Long before I heard from the man at the Division of Unclaimed Funds, I believed I had found whatever order and meaning I could in the lives of my father, brother, and mother, since their deaths separately had recalled, with a vividness that seemed greater than actual experience, everything that bound me to each. And the death of my mother had brought all three together into a relationship with me, the survivor, that was as satisfactory as possible, existing as it did as a feeling, generalized but not abstract, that transcribed the past into a kind of complex harmony. When at last I decided to look for the documents, I found them—luckily, almost at once—among the first papers in the top box on the closet shelf. I also found, just beneath those papers, a battered little book called "By Our Fireside: A Family Record," which contains, on its opening page, a signed certificate of my parents' first marriage. The following pages are intended for the names of the wedding guests and a description of the events of the wedding trip. Later sections are for drawings of the "family crest or coat of arms" of husband and wife and for their genealogical records, details about the births and adventures of the children, and so on. Many pages are simply titled "Noteworthy Events;" others, for "Wedding Anniversaries," have a subtitle that is partially blank: "Years married _____." The entries are mainly the work of my mother, written in a script whose appearance varies with the decades; in the early years my father sometimes amplifies her remarks.

Even while I was standing on the ladder in the closet, the book in my hand, I recognized that from her middle years on my mother had put down in it, often without comment, only matters of great importance to her. Except for two entries, all of those pages that were supposed to be devoted to "Noteworthy Events" are empty. Those entries are for the deaths of my father and brother. The latter—"Jack killed," followed by the date—was in a shaky script, for my mother was ninety-two, and living with us, when the accident happened: those blunt words were probably written later during that terrible morning on which I had lain next to her on her bed to tell her over and over the news I had been awakened some hours earlier to hear on the telephone. All her faculties were acute: not fearing in the slightest her own end, she simply found it difficult to believe that one of her children had preceded her.

*   *   *

I sat in my mother's upholstered rocker and read the record that I had not known she kept. Sitting in this chair on rainy summer mornings or days of winter storms, my mother looked for hours at the photographs on the opposite wall, perhaps hearing in them the melody or rhythms of her own past, for they consisted of pictures of her parents; of her sister and brother, who died before she came to live with us; of her young husband; and of Jack and me as babies, young boys, and adolescents.

Those pictures are now buried in one of the boxes, but I can see all of them, and two with particular clarity. In one, taken by my mother when I was thirteen, my father is combing my hair as I sit on the stone railing of the only house—a grand half-timbered English Tudor model, in a new subdivision of Little Rock—my parents ever owned. They owned it briefly—it was lost to the bank after my father deserted his family. In the picture my ankle is bandaged, and my brother is standing behind us, holding the .22 rifle he had secretly used his school lunch money to buy, his face swollen and his mouth tightly closed so that the space where he was missing teeth would not show. I have never liked this photograph; it reminds me not only of my father's imminent departure but of my own carelessness: sitting on the handlebars while Jack gave me a downhill ride on his bicycle, I let my foot become entangled in the spokes of the front wheel. The bicycle skidded to such a quick stop that my brother was hurled over me and landed on his jaw on the pavement, splintering his upper front teeth, a harbinger of that fatal accident four decades later in which he was hurled from the back seat into the dashboard of the limousine taking him and his crew—he was captain of a commercial airliner—from the Palmer House to O'Hare Airport.

The other is a photograph of my mother and me that my brother took the following summer, after the three of us, having no money and no other place to go, went a thousand miles north to knock, without advance notice, on the front door of the Ohio house of my mother's sister and her family. To help pay for our room and board there, Jack, who had just finished high school and hoped to enter college, found a job at a dime-store hamburger stand in downtown Cleveland. My mother joined my aunt in doing the washing and ironing she took in during those Depression years to augment her husband's meager salary, and I had a newspaper route to pay for my clothes and other personal expenses. The setting of this photograph is the Lake Erie island my uncle and aunt and their children visited for a week or so at the beginning of each summer season; a relative of my uncle's gave him the use of his house on the island in return for cleaning it and starting up the old car that was kept there. In this photograph, my mother and I are sitting on the stony beach, smiling at my brother; I am, at fourteen, already much larger than my mother, who was about five feet tall.

Surprisingly, she looks not much different in the photograph from the way she looked in her nineties, maybe because her hair, still brown in Little Rock, had turned to a pure white within the year. If in her last decades she seemed to me to appear much younger than her age, as a child I knew her to look much older than the mothers of my friends. For one thing, she was thirty-eight when I was born, and, for another, her wish not to spend money unnecessarily kept her from having a missing front tooth replaced (though, of course, she insisted at once on a bridge for

Jack). My father, who was thirteen years younger than she, had fallen in love with her when he was nineteen, and they were married when he was twenty; when he left her, after another nineteen years, for a younger woman, a widow who had inherited some money, my mother thought at first he had deserted her because of her missing tooth, and considered his departure her fault, for not having had it replaced. What I like about the photograph of the two of us on the beach is that my arm is around her shoulders and we both look happy.

* * *

Neither of my parents had much interest in their family trees, for my mother (except for the years of the divorce) lived for the present and my father always for the future, and so the pages in "By Our Fireside" for family crests and genealogical records are blank. In making her initial entries—those under "Wedding Guests" and "Our Wedding Trip"—my mother apparently felt the need to be faithful to certain of the book's demands; to explain the lack of names of wedding guests, for example, she wrote that she and Clayton, at least in the sense assumed by the book, "had no wedding—just went to church and were married." She went on, "My sister and Clayton's father [James, for whom I was named] only ones there. After wedding, sister went to station to meet [and here is inscribed the name of the man my aunt was later to marry], and Father came home and had dinner with us." There is no mention in that entry of what I once heard from my father: that at the dinner my grandfather said sternly to him, "Young man, you are at the table!" as he in his new happiness began to sing, or that my grandfather, then an insurance agent, had given the couple as a wedding present an insurance policy for which he had paid only the first month's premium—an unusually canny gift from a man who later, having come into some money, set up a loan agency, handed out to all clients whatever they wanted, until he had nothing left, and thenceforth lived with one or another of his children.

On the first of the pages for "Our Wedding Journey," my mother writes, much as she did for the wedding itself, "Had no wedding journey, but did have a pleasant little trip [from Cleveland] to Akron the day we were married"—a trip obviously made before the ceremony, probably so that my father could apply for a job, since they moved at once to Akron, where he became a laborer in the Goodyear plant. He held that job until he became a car salesman. Then—when he was about twenty-three—he was hired as the manager of the Cleveland Marmon agency, above whose showroom he had erected what a local newspaper referred to as "the largest advertising sign in the Western Hemisphere." (The yellowed clipping is buried in one of the boxes.) To my mother's comment about the lack of a wedding trip, my father adds a note the following summer, after a brief holiday from the Goodyear plant: "Saturday, July 1st, 1916, we took our 'wedding trip,' to Ruggles Grove, Huron, Ohio, where we ate, slept, and enjoyed ourselves for *two* days"—a vacation that, given the wages of a beginning laborer in that period, he had reason to boast of.

∗   ∗   ∗

A section of the book called "Where We Have Lived" has space for pictures of only three houses, their addresses, and dates of occupancy, so it is just as well that my mother made no attempt to fill in this part; my parents moved a number of times before my birth, and, during my childhood, at least once a year, to cities in the North, Midwest, and South. I began the first grade in P S

99 on Long Island, for my father then managed the Brooklyn
Studebaker agency, which might have had a smaller sign than did
the Cleveland Marmon agency but sold more automobiles than
any other Studebaker outlet in the country. Dissatisfied despite
his success, he quit to help establish Michelin-tire distributor-
ships throughout the eastern United States when that French
company made its first attempt to compete with American firms
in this country. He must have been an extraordinarily good
salesman, for, even after Michelin shrank back to France in the
early Depression years, he managed, in much the same sort of
position for various American tire firms, to increase both outlets
and sales. Once, as an explanation to me when I wondered at his
success, he gave me a book to read, *The Man Nobody Knows*, by
Bruce Barton, a New York advertising executive and United
States congressman, which finds Christ to be the greatest salesman of all time, able to win disciples through his belief in his
message. It was clear enough from his enthusiasm that my father
believed, if but briefly, in each product he sold, but he thought
that there was always a better product somewhere—one that
would enable him to find his "bracket."

Despite the injury he inflicted upon his family, particularly
upon his wife, I now think of him as both an innocent and the
quintessential American of his period, believing as he did that
one should look forward, never back, and that spiritual goals can
be achieved through material ends. His ever-unfulfilled spiritual
desires found a solace in organ music, which both he and my
mother liked above all other forms of art, and which even as a
child I thought to be crucial to the bond between them. In his
annual search for a new house, he always looked for one with a
fireplace, before which he could sit, an arm around my mother,

while they listened to organ-music records or, on the radio, those two popular organists of the day, Al Carney and Irma Glynn.

The lovely place he finally bought for us in Normandy, the fashionable Little Rock subdivision, was the closest approximation of his bracket that he ever found in a house, for it had, in addition to a fireplace, three bathrooms and a maid's room, this last large enough for Jack and me to play pool in, on the table my father bought us. But that house also represented one last, grandiose effort on my father's part, since by then the Depression had reached its lowest depth and even a superb salesman with the finest merchandise could find nobody to buy his wares.

On the Sundays that he was at home, he always took us to a Presbyterian church that he said had the finest pipe organ in the state of Arkansas. Early one Monday morning, he kissed us all goodbye, got into his Packard, and drove away from that English Tudor house in Normandy, never to return to it. Two weeks later, he telephoned my mother from San Antonio, to say that he had fallen in love with another woman and wanted a divorce; she didn't tell Jack or me anything about that call, though we knew, from the tears she couldn't hide, that she was concealing something dreadful. Within another week, she received a letter from the woman. Disturbed by the depth of her grief, I searched for it until I found it buried beneath stockings and undergarments in her bureau drawer. The last sentence read, "Obviously, if you love your husband as much as you say you do, you will agree to a divorce out of the knowledge that he finds a greater happiness with me."

Grace hated the word "obviously" for a number of years after that, because the logic of it in that sentence entrapped her—she *did* love Clayton, and so acquiesced in the divorce. His betrayal would have been less of a shock to her had he given at any time the slightest hint that he didn't love all of us as deeply as a husband and father ever loved his wife and their children.

*   *   *

In the "Wedding Anniversaries" section, my mother made four entries. Here are the first three:

YEARS MARRIED 10

Grand Ave., Wauwatosa, Wis. I met Clayton at office. We had dinner at the Sky Room in the Plankinton Hotel, then we went to the Palace. On the way to the hotel, in the auto, Clayton gave me a beautiful patent leather bag. He also sent me a lovely bunch of chrysanthemums. The prettiest bouquet I ever had.

YEARS MARRIED 15

We are living at 424 South Cedar St., Little Rock, Ark. Clayton gave me another bag. A pretty brown leather one. I still liked the one he gave me 5 years ago but it looked shabby beside the new one. Had a happy anniversary.

YEARS MARRIED 19

[By November 24th of this year, 1934, the divorce papers would have been filed. We had returned to Little Rock after stays in Fort Smith and Paducah, Kentucky.] 1801 North Arthur St., Little Rock, Ark. Clayton in Louisiana. Sent him the following telegram—

"Have had nineteen gloriously happy years *with* you. May the next nineteen be as happy *for* you. With all my love,

Your wife,

Grace"

At the bottom of this page, she adds, for herself alone, these words: "The *end*."

How strange it is, to be a man of sixty-three, married for forty years and the father of three grown sons, a man who carries in his memory what he considers to be the completed melody of the family he was born into—to be such a man, reading the words of a mother who, when she wrote them, was younger than he is now, and married not quite half as long! But for a moment that last entry brought me back to a time before the melody existed, to the years during which my father was not forgiven by me, and my brother was serving as a kind of surrogate for him, and I, as the younger son, was drawn, by our loss, into an ever-closer bond with my mother. In *Let Us Now Praise Famous Men,* James Agee finds it but a "small wonder" that in her "dry agony of despair a mother may fasten her talons and her vampire mouth upon the soul of her struggling son and drain him empty, light as a locust shell." This did not happen to me, perhaps because my mother kept her steadfast love for and loyalty to the absent Clayton, and lived always for the possibility of his return. Again and again, she spoke to me of the happiness and fulfillment that would come to me (as it did, as it does) in marriage—without such love, she said, life would be empty, sterile.

My brother was awarded a scholarship to General Motors Institute—an engineering college that augmented classroom studies with industrial experience—in Flint, Michigan, and my mother and I accompanied him there, hoping, vainly, that my father would send the small monthly sums of money that, in addition to the pay Jack received as a part-time worker in a spark-plug factory, would support us. Ultimately, my mother left for Cleveland to be a live-in maid for a well-to-do relative, while I, out of necessity, went to Chicago to stay with my father and stepmother, who were living beyond their means in a skyscraper apartment building on the Lake Shore. Apparently, they had already exhausted my stepmother's inheritance, for I saw at once a tension between them over the money she had brought to the marriage, and in the second month I was with them they were evicted from their luxurious suite for nonpayment of rent.

They moved into cheap quarters in a brick building on a streetcar line; it had but a single bedroom, which my stepmother insisted should be mine, even though she complained about the daybed in the living room. Whatever her motives, her generosity toward me made me feel guilty; even to smile at her was to me a betrayal of my mother. That Clayton had made his second wife unhappy seemed partly my responsibility, too, since I was his son. Sometimes at night I was awakened by the illusion that my mother was standing on the sidewalk beneath my open window, calling my name. My growing personal distress caused me to write the uncle and aunt who had taken in my mother and brother and me, to see if I could return; my aunt telephoned, telling me they loved me, and to come immediately.

Soon after I left, my stepmother divorced my father, and he continued his search for what even he at this period of his life must have recognized as unobtainable. Perhaps one who will not, or cannot, be sustained by the past, who has no present hope in his dreams, and yet whose lifelong habit is to be in motion, inevitably will move in the direction of self-destruction, toward a kind of willed defeat. My father drove his Packard south, to places where he was remembered in hotels as a valued customer. At one hotel near the Mexican border, he wrote a check for cash, using it to buy pesos, for he had heard that either the dollar or the peso was to rise in value in respect to the other, and he hoped to make a profit if he converted his currency the right way. But he converted it the wrong way. He had an insufficient sum in his bank account to cover that check, and so he drove blindly on, from city to city, staying at the best hotels and paying for his rooms with checks written on various nonexistent accounts. After six months of such frantic travel, he was, quite possibly to his relief, caught and sentenced to a three-year term at the Mansfield, Ohio, state reformatory. Upon the intercession of an industrialist grateful for his past services, he was paroled in less than a year, with the understanding that he would remarry Grace (she wrote, I know, a letter in his support), and with the requirement that he repay the hotels in accordance with an agreed-upon schedule. And so I was witness to my parents' second marriage— by the same clergyman who later, during my last furlough before being shipped overseas with my infantry division in the Second World War, was to marry Jean and me. My mother's final entry under "Wedding Anniversaries":

YEARS MARRIED _____
November 24, 1938. Married in Olmsted Falls, O. So very happy.

*   *   *

In reading the last two entries, I was surprised to discover that my parents were divorced for only four years—it means that they lived as husband and wife, usually in much harmony, for more than half a century. To me, those four years still seem a near-eternity, in which my adult nature was formed.

Despite my mother's happiness, my parents' new life together continued for several years to be troubled, for to the problems occasioned by the Depression were added those brought by the record of my father's recent past. He could not obtain, at first, any job other than as a manager of a used-car lot, his pay coming only from commissions. After much trying, he found a not much better position—one that again sent him from city to city with a salesman's valise. Since he was behind in those payments so necessary to his parole, my mother moved to a house belonging to a pair of unmarried sisters—friends of my parents from the time of their first marriage; in exchange for caring for the younger sister, who had cancer, she received free room and board for herself and for my father on weekends.

By this time, I was supporting myself while attending college by working nights as a copyboy for an afternoon Cleveland newspaper. I shared a large apartment with a reporter, a Lucky Strike salesman, and a middle-aged stenographer, and owned a secondhand car—I had paid my father a small sum for it while he was still at the used-car lot and thought I had given him the full price, but I discovered much later that he had paid out of his own pocket much more than I had given him. It was an example of a kindness that always existed within him (when, as a child, I developed a fondness for turtles, he picked them up from the highways, keeping them alive with food and water in his hotel rooms so that I could add them to my collection) but that his desertion had obscured from me.

My mother, of course, always saw that generous aspect of his character, her knowledge of it nourishing her love. She saw it even after, having found yet another woman of means, he telephoned my mother from a hotel in a central-Illinois town to ask for a second divorce. When she called me with that news, I cried, "That God-damned stupid son of a bitch," and for the only time I can remember she became angry with me, both for the sacrilege and for the attack on my father. I replied that he was at least stupid, since he needed her even more than she needed him, and that if he weren't stopped he'd end up in a greater mess than ever.

"What should we do, Jim?" my mother asked me. "He wants me to phone him tomorrow night."

"Pack your bag," I said. "I'll be at your place at six in the morning."

"What about Yvonne?"

"To hell with Yvonne. . . . No, I don't mean that. Tell her sister to take care of her or to find somebody else."

It rained throughout our journey. Neither of us spoke much, though occasionally my mother reached for my hand, and smiled at me. She was so small that I felt during that strange trip more like her father than her son. I was chiefly worried about what I would do if there was a woman with my father in the hotel room; I thought I would ask her to leave. But what if she wouldn't? At the hotel, I took my mother's bag, found out my father's room number, and escorted her to it. The door opened to my knock; my father was alone. "Here's your wife," I said, dropping the bag and pushing her so quickly into his arms that his embrace of her was part of his moment of astonishment; and then I ran down-stairs to my car. It was still raining. I turned on the radio; Joe Louis was fighting somebody, I'm not sure who—though I do know that I was wrong, years later, in telling my parents that while they resolved their problems successfully enough to have decades of happiness, I was listening as Louis defeated Max Schmeling in fifteen rounds. All I really remember is that some-time after the fight ended my father was standing on the sidewalk in the rain, tapping at my closed and steamy window. "Grace is spending the night, and I've reserved a room for you," he said, pretending it was the rain that made him rub his eyes as he turned away. "I don't know why I've been a fool so long. Thanks for bringing her."

* * *

My life remained entwined with that of my parents, for, when the other occupants left my Cleveland apartment, my mother and father moved in. Upon my induction into the Army, they made it wholly their own, and they lived there for fifteen years—their longest stay at one address. During the war, my father operated a turret lathe in a defense plant. He joined the union and became a shop steward. One afternoon he lost part of a thumb to his machine but was back at work the following morning. When the war ended, he returned to salesmanship, and my mother became a bookkeeper for a painting contractor. She liked the job—particularly the task of making out checks for the painting crew. (Perhaps she enjoyed that task too much. Once, while the owner was out of town, she mailed a small Christmas bonus to all the painters, because, in her opinion, they deserved it, and the books she kept led her to know the company could readily afford such a present. Upon his return, the owner indignantly demanded that she recall all the checks. He waited until the following year to institute Christmas bonuses as a company policy.) At holiday times, the apartment would become crowded, for both Jack and I brought our families. I think of the decade and a half that my parents lived in the Cleveland apartment as a particularly fulfilling period for them, one in which my father at last was able to separate his domestic life from his dreams. That is to say, he was happy at home and faithful in his affections. He was still restless enough outside it to change jobs as rapidly as ever, but my strongest recollection of those years is of rooms

[42]

filled with laughter and talk and the smells of cinnamon and yeasty cloverleaf rolls.

In his later years, my father's eagerness to have at last a business of his own led him to a final error in judgment. He bought a Kaiser-Frazer dealership in Ashtabula, Ohio, at the time that car manufacturer was failing. I was teaching in Kentucky then—it was my first full-time position—and Jean had given birth to our second son. Her mother had recently died, and she had inherited a couple of thousand dollars. Since we needed a new car, we thought we'd drive up to Ashtabula, to help my father's new business along by buying one from him. My parents were living, temporarily, in the single house along a particular, and most pleasant, section of Lake Erie shoreline that had not been boarded up. (The whole area was soon to be razed for industrial development.) As we pulled into the driveway, I saw my mother smiling at us from a little swing my father had just hung from an apple bough for our older child; it was mid-May. Some apple blossoms—reddened by a sun disappearing into the lake—had fallen on her shoulders and hair, and the sense of the transience of all things saddened me.

Instead of selling us a car, my father sold us two thousand dollars' worth of stock in his new company, for he needed the money to meet his payroll. I believe he thought he was doing us a favor; he was optimistic, and had any number of ingenious plans for making the business profitable. When the Internal Revenue Service locked the company's doors, Jean and I worried that, as stockholders, we might be held liable for some of the debts. But my father, proud of the good credit rating that he had struggled over the years to gain and that had enabled him to buy the dealership, refused to enter bankruptcy, convincing both the bank and the I R S—much as he once had the parole board—of his ability to repay his debts; he was almost seventy before he paid the last of them.

Several months before my father showed the initial symptoms of cancer, my family and I visited my parents in Olmsted Falls; they had returned to the town of their second wedding to share a house with my mother's now widowed sister. During that visit, my mother took me aside to say that Clayton was worried that I had never forgiven him for his treatment of his family so many years ago; and she added, almost wistfully, "I hope, Jimmy, that he's wrong." I said, with indignation, that the courage and determination he had displayed over the years made me proud to be his son. But it was less his anxiety than her uncertainty about my ability to forgive that rankled me, and made my response close to an angry one. Though she never knew it, the seemingly infinite nature of her own mercy was a formidable quality, against which the other members of her family were forced to measure themselves; and if, at this moment, I felt defensive before that quality in her, what effect had it had upon my father in his transgressions? Since in our conversations neither he nor I ever brought up the subject of those painful years, I had thought his apparent obliviousness of them a continuing indication of a faulty or selective memory. Until she spoke to me that day of his feelings, I had not realized that he could be so vulnerable to the past to sense in me, through those subtle and unspoken ways in which family members can communicate with each other, a coldness or wariness I had refused to acknowledge in myself.

His dreams, though, remained invulnerable. While recovering from his first cancer operation, he made plans for a new business, and was still dreaming of the future at the time of his second operation. My mother, who was then about ninety, nursed him after both surgeries. The injustices and sufferings visited upon him by his illness became one in my mind with those he had visited upon his family so long ago, and I found I had truly forgiven him. Intimacy, like disdain, needs no words, and I believe he understood that I had been released from a burden I had been stubbornly carrying for decades.

Jean and I were with my parents, to celebrate my father's birthday and their twin wedding anniversaries, on the day he died. His last words were a defiant denial of reality: "I don't have cancer!" he cried, shortly after the blood began to gush from his mouth. Despite that nadir following his second wife's departure, he was no Willy Loman, and the indomitable nature of his dreams gave him a victory of spirit over death itself.

Tucked between the pages of "By Our Fireside" is a note—undated, without either salutation or signature—that my mother wrote to my father. From her handwriting, and from the references to the sunset and to my brother and me, I can attribute that note to the days after my parents left Ashtabula for an Akron apartment and my father was managing a dismal bureau of women who sold subscriptions to *Life* and *Time* through telephone solicitations; the words are my mother's way of letting him know that the loss of his business is of no consequence to her:

The view from our home was most wonderful at all times but when the sun was setting and the sky a riot of gorgeous colors, what more could one ask for when beauty so satisfied the soul? Of course to hear Al Carney or Irma Glynn play the organ happiness is complete especially when you have a true lover husband and two fine young boys who bid fair to become well

known in their chosen life work. To me boys and girls are
wondrous with their youth, beauty, and enthusiasm. Roses
round the door, babies on the floor, may sound soothing and
sweet but I prefer them grown as our boys are. I have always
preferred them as they were, tiny or big. This is my heart
throb. See ya in the morning.

That note would have been written in the mid-fifties, many
years after Al Carney and Irma Glynn had ceased their radio
broadcasts; so my mother's preference for a given moment of her
family present over any moment in the past was strengthened—
even made possible—by her ability to carry into the present
those values kept within her memory: sunsets of the immediate
past and organ music of a more distant time. We tend to think
of youth as flexible, and of age as rigid, but this is more a matter
of bones than of psyches: as any longtime teacher knows, youth,
always looking forward, can break before those unexpected
tragedies to which age, looking back, only bends.

In her last decade with us, Grace possessed an extraordinary
inner suppleness. On the dreadful morning that I had to tell her
of my brother's death, she said, "Jackie," remembering him as the
laughing child who on more than one occasion had slipped away
from her after a bath or soaking himself with a garden hose to
go running, naked and wet, down the street—an event I found
faithfully recorded under "The Children" section of her book. If
memories of this sort at first intensify one's sense of loss, they
serve as an ultimate solace, much as do pictures on a wall.

Fortunate in the possession of sharp eyesight as well as hearing, my mother enjoyed wandering over the large back lawn on
pleasant summer days, finding so many four-leaf clovers (neither

Jean nor I ever found any) that they became miniature bouquets in cream pitchers or shot glasses on the dining-room table. Certain of our linguistic tendencies, including a gift for word-play, can develop with age; a sip of wine at dinner enabled her to make puns the dexterity of which I could not match until I had drunk three full glasses. She liked the summer visits that Bill, Jean's father, paid us nearly every year until his death. Although he had a pacemaker and suffered from emphysema, he smoked cigarette after cigarette. "Don't smoke," she would tell him as he reached for his pack at the breakfast table. He would grumble, "That's my gracious Gracie, always cracking the whip," and she would respond, "Somebody has to, bilious Bill," and they would both laugh, and he would put away his cigarettes for a while.

Her age allowed her—it was the only advantage she made of it—to say whatever was on her mind. When Larry, our oldest son, brought home from Philadelphia the young black woman he planned to marry, I worried that Grace, though I had never known her to display prejudice of any kind, might say something inappropriate. My mother was asleep by the time the two of them arrived, so the meeting occurred the next morning. Larry was frying bacon as his wife-to-be entered the kitchen, where Grace was sipping her coffee.

"Hello, I'm Jackie," the young woman said.

"That was the name of my older son," my mother said.

Jackie said sympathetically, "I know."

"And you're Larry's girl?"

"Yes."

"Do you love him?"

"Yes. Very much."

Perhaps feeling that such questioning might be making her

nervous, Larry told Jackie to take an egg from the refrigerator. As she was bringing it to the stove, Grace said to her, "That egg looks beautiful in your hand."

Since my mother refused to take seriously any questions about her health, Jean and I found it difficult to tell if she ever was ill. One November night a few weeks before her hundredth birthday, she mysteriously slipped into a coma; we called for an ambulance to take her to the hospital. The next day, I found her in much the same condition—unconscious, or too deeply asleep to respond to my presence or words except by a barely perceptible flick of the eyelids; she was receiving oxygen and glucose through plastic tubes. While I was sitting by her bedside, her doctor arrived. He said that twice during the night she had come out of her sleep to pull the tubes loose, as if she wanted to get through her dying as quickly as possible. I said that such a wish ought to be respected, but he replied that there was a slim chance that the results of some lab tests he had ordered might provide him with a clue that could lead to her recovery.

I sat there for maybe four hours, thinking of how remote and childlike she seemed, and of how, in pulling out the life-support systems, she was behaving as I had guessed she would while I was writing a novel several years earlier. It may seem absurd that a man in his late fifties, as I was at the time I began that novel, would be worried about the grief he expected to suffer over the death of a mother thirty-eight years older than himself—a woman whose life had long since seemed as nearly complete as it could get—but one of my reasons for writing that manuscript was to imagine, as best I could, how a woman like her would die, and the effect that her death would have on a son somewhat like me, so that I would be prepared for the actual moment. Since she didn't die on this occasion, it, like the novel, was an aid to me when death did come, about six weeks later—death that, in the manner of its occurrence, brought me more happiness than I would have believed possible had I not already attributed some such feeling to the middle-aged son of my fiction.

Early on the second morning of my mother's hospital stay, her doctor phoned to say that she had made what seemed to him a remarkable recovery—for it had been without treatment of any kind—and that she was her alert former self and probably could go home in a day or so. (On the previous night, as I later was to be told, a nurse came out of my mother's room to say in astonishment to a colleague, "That dying old woman just spoke to me. I was checking to see how well she was breathing, and I whispered, 'See you later,' thinking she was comatose and wouldn't hear me even if she weren't, and she whispered back at me, 'Alligator.'")

And so she lived to greet her grandchildren and great-grand-children on her hundredth birthday, to drink a small glass of champagne, and to munch on a piece of birthday cake. She could eat only soft foods, for an orderly at the hospital in obeying the regulation to remove the false teeth of all bed patients, had accidentally broken off the single natural tooth that kept her upper dental plate in place—the plate that, when she finally consented to having it made, filled in all the gaps in her front teeth. On the snowy day in the second week of December that she once again suddenly became comatose, I entered her bed-room to check on her condition; I was hoping, really, that she would die in her own bed before the ambulance arrived. Some-how, she knew I was there; she opened her eyes, groped for my hand, and gave me the most radiant (and the gummiest) smile that a son ever received from a dying parent. As I have said, my father's last words were "I don't have cancer!"; my mother's, which followed that smile, were "I love you."

*   *   *

My parents' appreciation of organ music traced back to their pleasure in the melodies played on the organs of the silent- and early talking-picture houses as well as on those of their childhood churches, and so their taste in music written or arranged for that instrument was not circumscribed. They delighted in tunes by Irving Berlin, including "Alexander's Ragtime Band" and "Always"; songs of the American West and South; lighthearted Depression ditties such as "Keep Your Sunny Side Up"; Viennese and American waltzes; Schubert's "Ave Maria"; and traditional hymns like "O God, Our Help in Ages Past." They enjoyed the humming in the organ pipes of virtuoso performances of "Flight of the Bumble Bee" and another kind of resonance to be found in Bach and Handel and Mozart.

What a mélange of tunes, unified only by the instrument upon which each piece was played! I suppose that memory, like the organ, is an instrument capable of infusing the most secular music with spiritual sounds. Despite the sadness in some of its chords, the melody of the family I was born into reverberates in my memory as if Al Carney and Irma Glynn are rendering on dual organs a song of such steadfast hope (his console) and such steadfast love (hers) that it ends up as a hallelujah.

1987

✑Heroes
Among the
Barbarians

FIFTEEN YEARS AGO, an alienated fellow citizen, a Vietnam veteran living in a rusty trailer several miles from my Finger Lakes farmhouse, gave me, in return for my posting bail following his arrest for shoplifting several cans of tuna fish from an Ithaca supermarket, a four-volume set of *The Documentary History of the State of New-York* that had belonged to his mother, now dead. The books were published in 1850–51, the documents arranged by E. B. O'Callaghan, MD, under the direction of the Honorable Christopher Morgan, Secretary of State. Here I found English translations of the papers relating to Frontenac's 1696 expedition into my region (a piece of land jutting into Cayuga Lake not far from my home is named for that French count and colonial governor in North America). His campaign was directed against the Iroquois; the translated accounts were written by young French aristocrats and others from the field, and presumably were sent back to the French court. "The Count is already advised," begins the opening paper,

> *by despatches at the departure of last year's ships, of the*
> *preparations for a considerable expedition against the Iroquois*
> *and principally against the Onnontagues which is the chief*
> *nation, where the councils of the other five are held, the most*
> *devoted to the English, and the most strenuously opposed to*
> *the negociations for peace of preceding years. It became of*
> *importance to crush them, and it appeared to many more*
> *advantageous to do so during the winter inasmuch as it was*
> *certain, said they, to find in the Village at least all the women*
> *and children who being destroyed or captured would draw*
> *down ruin on the warriors or oblige them to surrender to us.*

How rational, how brutally cold, such calculations! I first read these accounts on a winter evening, sitting before a log fire in the living room of my Greek Revival farmhouse; the warmth of the fire, as well as the distance separating me from the struggle for colonial domination by European powers in the French and Indian Wars, permitted me the luxury of irony toward the scribes, those refined young men who doubly protected their sensibilities: first by giving to informed opinion the responsibility for the slaughter or enslavement of women and children while the warriors (I supposed) were off hunting, and then (as was obvious from other papers) by referring to all Indians, regardless of the side they supported, as savages or barbarians. The scribes found it painfully difficult to acknowledge that an Iroquois, even one whose behavior they admired, might possess the nobility or courage of a Frenchman, as the following account of the capture of an Onondaga fort reveals:

*The grain and the rest of the booty consisting of pots, guns,
axes, stuffs, wampum belts, and some peltries were plundered
by our Frenchmen and Savages. The destruction of the Indian
corn was commenced the same day, and was continued the
two following days. The grain was so forward that the stalks
were very easily cut by the sword and sabre without the least
fear that any could sprout again. Not a single head remained.
The fields stretched from a league and a half to two leagues
from the fort: The destruction was complete. A lame girl was
found concealed under a tree, and her life was spared.*

*An old man, also captured, did not experience the same fate.
M. le Comte's intention, after he had interrogated him, was to
spare his life on account of his great age, but the savages who
had taken him and to whom he was given were so excited that
it was not deemed prudent to dissuade them from the desire
they felt to burn him. He had, no doubt, prepared himself
during his long life to die with firmness, however cruel the
tortures he should have to endure. Not the slightest complaint
escaped his lips. On the contrary he exhorted those who
tormented him to remember his death, so as to display the
same courage when those of his nation would take vengeance
on them; and when a savage, weary of his harangues, gave
him some cuts of a knife, "I thank thee," he cried, "but thou
oughtst to complete my death by fire. Learn, French dogs! and
ye, savages! their allies—that ye are the dogs of dogs.
Remember what ye ought to do, when you will be in the same
position as I am." Similar sentiments will be found perhaps to
flow rather from ferociousness than true valour; but there are
heroes among barbarians as well as among the most polished
nations, and what would be brutality in us may pass for
valour with an Iroquois.*

[55]

* * *

When my wife and I bought our farmhouse, in 1962, we could afford only thirty-eight acres of the surrounding fields and woods. Though that might seem more than adequate for a family with no intention of farming who had previously lived in a series of apartments and houses on city lots, I wanted proprietorship of the entire one hundred and seventy-three acres that had belonged to the farm almost from the time it had become private property. During the American Revolution, the Iroquois remained loyal to their British allies, and as a consequence the Continental Congress sent a punitive force under the command of General John Sullivan into our region, its swath of Indian villages and fields so thorough that the Iroquois were routed forever. After the War of 1812, the federal government divided the region into parcels as payment for the service of soldiers in that second struggle against the British (a conflict initiated by our young nation chiefly from the desire to gain more land from them as well as from Indians in the Northwest). Most of the veterans sold their tracts to land speculators who sold them in turn to farmers like Thomas Kelsey, the one who had built the house that now was ours.

Through luck, a small equity, and a good lawyer, we managed, within a few years, to gain back everything that had belonged to Thomas Kelsey and those who had followed him. But I was surprised to find that the rewritten mortgage didn't give me the satisfaction I had been counting on. Maybe if I had worked that land, as generations before me had, I would have felt myself a valid inheritor of the soil; as it was, though, simple ownership wasn't enough. Thinking that knowledge of the past might give me rightful possession, I became a restless amateur archaeologist, searching for signs of earlier human habitation on our own and nearby land. Not much more than a mile from our front door, an Indian village once prospered; another, an additional mile down a little-used gravel road, is still commemorated by a deteriorating state historical marker (a relic itself, from the days in which families took leisurely weekend drives in their new Fords or Studebakers) as an "Immense Early Iroquois Site." The marker goes on to say that remnants of a circular palisade enclose a pond—neither of which I have ever been able to discern. The Indians found the clay here suitable for pottery; possibly this site was in use before the establishment of the Iroquois Confederacy. The one closer to our home is of later origin, and surely would have been a village like those destroyed by Frontenac and Sullivan. According to various books I have read, it would have contained a "long house" serving both as communal dwelling and metaphor for the family of nations, as well as a sacred tree whose roots were held to knit together the cosmos within which that larger family dwelt. Unlike one of my sons, who found not only arrowheads but a stone knife with its edge still sharp, I came across no Indian artifacts, but I did discover many signs of my white predecessors on our own and adjacent property.

The earliest map of my county that I have seen indicates that a sawmill once stood by the creek a half-mile down the dirt road from our house, which also is located on the map; here the logs would have been taken to be transformed into the planks and joists and siding from which the house was constructed in 1831, as the fields were being cleared. At first, I thought the sawmill could have operated only intermittently, for, though the creek it depended upon for power never dries up, it is a silver serpent between rocky pools in the dry months, and only after a two-day spring or autumnal downpour can I hear it from our porch roaring like a distant freight train. While engaged in an early exploration, I was delighted to find, on the little hill above the creek, the eroded remnants of a previous road that curved away from the present one, and the rounded embankments of an earthen dam (the center of which has long since washed away) upon which the earlier road had been built. From the contours of the terrain, I could tell that the dam would have backed up enough water to make a millpond covering the quarter-mile to the woods, part of which now belonged to my family.

Deep within those woods, the creek divides; up one of those branches I discovered the twin embankments of what must have been a much earlier dam—one less difficult to build, the ravine here being deep but narrow. The cart trail to it is a pair of mossy channels, discernible only on the slope; on the forested ground above the ravine, the trail has been erased by what appear to be shallow bomb craters in the loam. Actually, as I came to realize, these depressions are a consequence of the ripping out of huge tree-root systems, in a wholly natural process. The topsoil in this area of the woods is a thin covering over an almost impervious clay, causing the roots of the hard maples, oaks, pines, and beeches to spread out just beneath the surface; were there boulders for the roots to fasten around or into, as there are on the slopes of the ravine, the trees would still have managed to withstand high winds. Given the geological conditions, though, the trees most successful in outdistancing the others in the race to the sky are the ones to topple in the winter gales.

That portion of the ravine containing the old dam is almost at the center of a square mile whose borders are the country roads, and hence is as secluded a place as my neighborhood provides. Just downstream from the dam the ravine widens into a glen, with a little swamp at one end. Though not even a puckered hole remains to indicate a fruit cellar, a line of decaying stumps and a haphazard assortment of withered apple and cherry trees in that glen, no doubt volunteers from an original orchard, indicate that a settler had a cabin nearby. The spongy cart channels, the remains of the dam, the stumps and gnarled volunteers, seem part of the fading impress of memory upon the wrinkled surface of the mind of the *Terra Mater* worshiped by Indians; indeed, on the hill on the other side of the creek—that boundary of my family's domain—two long and curving mounds or banks of earth long ago were built for a purpose obscure enough to me that I decided at once those banks to be sacred Iroquoian earthworks.

* * *

It was within the glen itself that, on a spring afternoon twenty years ago, I experienced, with my wife, Jean, and our five-year-old son, Jimmy, a moment of such extraordinary happiness that it should have ended forever my search for whatever was required to give my mortgage its necessary spiritual seal. We had been marking, with strips of red cloth knotted around the still bare saplings and tree limbs, the best route for the trail we were planning to make through the woods that summer. Jean and I had left a note on the front door for our two older sons upon their return home by school bus, telling them that if they wished to find us they should follow those red strips into the woods. I sat with Jean and Jimmy, the three of us hidden in a bed of weeds in the glen, listening to the ever-closer cries of the older boys as they came across each new token of our whereabouts. As we heard not only their shouts but the nearby crackling of under-brush, Jimmy's eyes began to glow with the anticipation that Jean and I also felt; and, at the instant before they found us, I knew the kind of love for family that resonates against love for place, with family imposing value on land even as land, the Earth itself, grants value to the intertwining human lives.

To commemorate this moment, as well as to establish an observation post over the secret heart of a territory that now seemed to belong more firmly to me, I built (once Jimmy was old enough to be my assistant) a tree house with a porch over-looking the creek and its glen. We constructed this cozy home between two tall beeches—survivors of storm because their roots are anchored in boulders, survivors of saws and axes because beech (until the scarcity of other kinds of lumber raised its value) was considered a worthless wood. Though the Indians who might have built the mounds on the opposing slope would have considered *my* cosmos pretty small, they would have un-derstood that a playhouse in the trees might serve as a metaphor for it.

That was what I thought, while enjoying the work with my son high in the leafy beeches. One holds on to a poignant spiritual experience by commemorating it with a structure, but what happens when the fun of hammering is over? Jimmy wanted to build a second tree house in a neighboring maple, connecting the two with a suspension bridge, while I thought of dredging the swamp to make a forest pool for bathing. No, I wasn't quite satisfied with what I had, not yet. In later months and years, while sitting in a folding lawn chair on the porch of that tree house and looking toward the creek and the opposite slope, I thought that what I still lacked was the ownership of the property containing the mounds, significant with mystery as they were. The bearded proprietor of that and much other land lived a couple of miles away on the state highway, where he ran a junkyard. Maybe the desire he saw in my eyes when I inquired about the purchase of a strip of real estate adjoining my own raised its worth to him. Like me, he wasn't about to sell off a section of his property to anybody. No doubt he would have bought part or all of mine, had he been able to. I guess that, in our separate ways, both of us were land speculators, hoping for an eventual increase in the value of what we already had or hoped to gain.

* * *

On three or four occasions in my life, I have been strongly drawn to strangers, probably because they seem to me projections of the self I would like to be. Marcos (I never learned his last name) is one of this number. I met him only once, and for less than a couple of hours. The encounter took place nine years ago, while I was vacationing in Greece with Jean and Jimmy in the summer preceding that youngest son's entrance into college.

As part of our month-long exploration of Greece, we spent a week on Crete; it was here that we came across Marcos, the guard and caretaker at Gournia, whose partially excavated ruins (he told us) are the most "real," being the least tampered with, of all the Minoan sites on that island. We had rented a car at Heraklion to travel about Crete, and with it visited such major Minoan ruins as the palaces at Knossos, Phaistos, and Zakro, as well as the legendary birthplace of Zeus at the bottom of a cave that went like a mineshaft deep into a mountain. ("Baby Zeus here," our guide into the cave said, pointing to a damp ledge and cradling his arms to suggest a sleeping infant.) Perhaps because no attempts at reconstruction have been made, Gournia is not a popular tourist site; we came upon it by chance about 8 P.M. while on our return to our hotel at Agios Nikolaos after a day's swimming and sunbathing at the beach at Vai—Jean happened to glance at the stones rising up a hill a short distance from the highway, and, because it was too early for any Greek restaurateur to be serving dinner, we stopped.

Except for Marcos, wearing his guard's cap and sitting on a wall at the very top of the hill, the site was deserted. We wandered around, not knowing what to look for, until he approached us; he resembled, I thought, the white-bearded, older Hemingway.

"How do you like our little town?" he asked, as serious as he was polite; and then, without waiting for an answer, took us on an extended tour, showing us the altar—with its groove for the ax, the drain for the blood of sacrificed animals, and the stone for grain-offerings to the gods—and the other ruins, explaining, as we walked, the function of each building, and how all of them had been constructed to withstand minor earth tremors. He had been guard and caretaker here for years, he said; he and his wife lived in a house, hidden behind the hill, where they had raised their son and three daughters. One of the daughters now worked at the excavations at Zakro. In giving us the history of the digging at Gournia, Marcos used "we" and "our" whenever he spoke of the decisions and findings of the archaeologists, even those whose research preceded his arrival; until I recognized the degree of his interest and involvement, I thought his use of pronouns the consequence of an uncertain command of English. (A travel agent in Agios Nikolaos told us the next day we were lucky to have been shown the site by Marcos, for he knew far more about it than did any of the licensed guides: "Marcos not only knows, he cares," she said.)

He knew, certainly, and with a scope far greater than any study of my woods had provided me, of nature's ability to destroy both her own works and those of man: he spoke not only of the shiftings of the land that over the millennia had sent parts of Gournia under the sea, but of the 1956 quake he had lived through. At eleven o'clock one May morning, he heard the earth make a sound—"It went 'mmmm,'" he said—and that murmur was followed by intense tremors and a tidal wave. The fresh-water pool connected to the harbor at Agios Nikolaos turned yellow and then black, and all the fish died; for that deep pool, according to Marcos, was a window of the volcano on Santorini which, about 1500 B.C., exploded in the cataclysm that destroyed the Minoan civilization.

And then he spoke of the Eteo-Cretans, small people with oval eyes (one happened to pass by on a bicycle as we talked), who originally came to Crete from Anatolia, the Asian part of modern Turkey, and who claim to be descendants of the Minoans. To most Greeks we had met, any mention of Turkey would have been followed by a reference to Turks as historic plunderers of Greece, savage aggressors upon another's soil, the conflict over Cyprus being the contemporary instance; but Marcos ignored the opportunity. "The Eteo-Cretans tell the rest of us on Crete, 'We brought you the Light,' because their ancestors came from the East," he said.

As he was answering our questions—and we had many, for no guide had so stimulated our desire for knowledge—a line of tiny flames, which for some time had been gradually moving up a distant hillside like a row of red-coated soldiers, burst at midpoint into a pillar of fire. "It is very dry," Marcos said. "It is sad that so many olive and almond trees will burn"; but then a bell began to ring from his hidden house, and he smiled. "That is my wife calling me to dinner. We eat early, an American custom: all the archaeologists here have been Americans."

Not wanting him to leave quite yet, I asked him how many languages he spoke. "Seven altogether," he said. "In my house, I speak Greek, of course. Here on the site I speak mainly English, German, French, or Italian, and know them best. But I can speak Swedish and, less well, Japanese. I learn my languages from the people who visit Gournia; they don't know they are teaching me while I am teaching them." He paused to watch the conflagration. "Look, the flames are dying. The firefighters from Agios Nikolaos have arrived. . . . Gournia is my home, but it is not mine more than it is another's. It belongs to all who have come to it, which is why I try so hard to learn their languages. It belongs to the Eteo-Cretans, though they don't come. It belongs to the past, which I also try to know, as best I can." He took off his cap to rub the sweat from his forehead, and then looked, for the longest moment, at that cap. "Sometimes," he said, "I wonder where I will go."

"You're near retirement?" I asked. "You must leave Gournia?"

"Oh, no, no, no," he said, vigorously shaking his head. "What I mean is, where will my soul go, when I die? But it is a foolish worry, for I don't think there is a heaven—certainly not one divided into areas according to the different languages." The bell clanged sharply. "I am not a considerate husband," he said. "Even the bell becomes angry. Goodbye," and he shook hands with each of us.

I took out my wallet, to pay for our guided tour here as I had elsewhere, but Marcos backed away. "Our little Gournia has no proper tourist facilities, no kiosk for cigarettes and postcards and souvenirs," he said, with an ironic sweep of his hand that suggested his pleasure in the fact. "I want no gratuity," and, turning, he bounded up the hill like a man half his age, waved his cap to us from the crest, and vanished.

*   *   *

Like "hero," their epithet for the quasi-divine dead, "barbarian" is a word that comes from the ancient Greeks, who used it to differentiate others from themselves, all those others who didn't speak in the civilized and rational measures of the native tongue and whose words sounded in Athenian ears as the unintelligible "bar-bar." As word and political concept for freedom, "democracy" also comes from the Greeks, and they were thus the first to invoke its name in justification of questionable territorial claims or of simple domination ("hegemony" is yet another word we owe to them) over not only the barbarians but some who shared their own language.

During a recent rainsquall, a dead limb dropped upon the tree house I had built so many years ago, putting a hole in its Fiberglas roof. While walking the half-mile through the woods to the tree house, carrying a roll of duct tape and a bucket of roof patch for the repairs, I found myself thinking about those etymologies in connection with the Iran-Contra affair, still very much in the news, the revelations of activities both legal and illegal frequently being justified, even glorified, by our highest officials through the use of such Greek terms; and with a P B S documentary I had watched some weeks earlier that dealt with the way the populace of any given nation will praise its own warriors while turning its enemies—its ideological opponents, its rivals for territory—into abstractions, the better to kill them.

A decade ago, I would not have thought of etymologies or sociopolitical matters while engaged in such a seemingly nostalgic task as repairing a tree house I had built with a young son. I've heard it said that all of us, as we age, tend in our thinking to replace the concrete or the real (the world of human relationships) with intellectual or moral abstractions—not, of course, to murder what has mattered most to us in the past, but probably as part of our attempt to get a handle on life during the period of our gradual disengagement from our identities as parents and workers. In any event, while I was balancing on my toes on the tree house's porch railing in the attempt to reach a gouge in the roof I couldn't see, my mind was less on my task or my personal experiences or even on the twenty-foot drop to the glen than it was on notions of possession and hegemony. Initially, my thoughts were on the Iroquois (whose Confederacy became one of the models for our Constitution) and their view of a natural cosmos too sacred to be owned by any nation or mortal. Then I found myself comparing the long-ago destruction, in my neighborhood, of Iroquois villages and their inhabitants in conflicts for possession by larger rival powers, with the current ravaging of Nicaraguan villages by our Contras and whatever "good" Indians could be coerced into the democratic cause, the pillagers now being praised as freedom fighters or the moral equivalent of our Founding Fathers for their efforts to topple a legitimate, if Marxist-oriented, government in defense of our hegemony in Central America. Against all that, I put what I could: a remembered account of the bravery of an old Iroquois undergoing torture as well as my personal memory of a caretaker on Crete, and his view of the ownership of some ruins he loved.

As for me, I understood only then how fully I had lost—along with certain other passions with which it no doubt was connected, as it is throughout our animal kingdom—the territorial desire, which in mankind alone is typically justified as spiritual or ideological in nature; and, as a corollary loss, the belief in any possible relationship between owning and loving or even knowing. But how I had yearned, at one time, to possess more land,

and then just a bit more—the latter so that I could own a pair of nondescript mounds of unknown origin that my imagination had made sacred!

These are the sort of abstract things a man of sixty-five is apt to think about or remember, while in the process of acknowledging to himself that he is presently engaged in a pretty foolish and irresponsible activity—in my case, going out without a partner into the woods to teeter upon a slippery railing in order to patch the roof of an observation post over territory I no longer would or even could claim as mine alone, except in a dry and legal sense.

Afterwards, though, sitting on the cot in the snug little room and looking upward at my patch, I was glad to see that I had successfully sealed the hole. Our children are grown and either away from home or too occupied with the business of life to spend a night in the tree house, but Jean and I still on occasion do; it is a good feeling to sit here before a candle in the forest dark, drinking wine until we get drowsy and a bit tipsy, and then to wake in the morning in the tree limbs, hearing the twitter of birds and the murmur of water over stones, and—if we are lucky—seeing a deer or two walk the trail they have made that goes between the pair of beeches (and so the deer pass directly beneath our feet!) before wending down the hill to the creek. The "No Trespassing" signs we once posted at the edge of the woods have long since disappeared, some of them torn down by hunters. Even if the tree house no longer marks the heart of a private cosmos, it still overlooks a spot made as holy by personal experience as any piece of real estate can be for adherents of no particular faith in these final decades of a century that still can't find the answer to history's persistent and ever-more-desperate question.

ᶜⁿContextual
Surprises

O N   A   J U N E   D A Y   in 1956, my wife, Jean, and I en-
trusted our children to a neighbor and left our home
in eastern Kentucky to look for another in the Finger
Lakes region of New York; after six years of teaching at a small
college in the hills of the Cumberland National Forest, I had
been appointed an assistant professor at Cornell. We stopped in
Cleveland to visit a friend—a colleague of mine during my first
teaching job—who was convalescing at a mental hospital; Kent
had suffered a breakdown following the unexpected death of the
woman he had expected to marry. When a nurse unlocked the
door to admit us to his ward, two patients playing table tennis in
the hallway raised their paddles to menace us or to defend
themselves; obviously we were interlopers in the bastion of their
emotional security.

Kent, who had been expecting us, stood before his door in an
outsized hospital robe, smiling. He gave Jean a kiss and me a

warm handshake before ushering us into the room and intro-
ducing us to his roommate, Gordon, a frail and balding man in
his early thirties whose initial shyness toward us quickly turned
to curiosity and signs of friendship.

Gordon sat at the very edge of his mattress like a fragile and
eager-eyed bird, listening to us talk, interrupting our conversation now and then to offer us cookies from a plastic package. The
gentle irony that always characterized Kent was so evident it
seemed to me he was merely acting the role of mental patient;
he told us, for example, that the crucial aspect of his therapy lay
less in psychiatry and antidepressant drugs than in the baseball
game he was daily forced to endure, an activity so boring that he
was recovering his sanity as quickly as possible to escape it.
Patients hid in closets or under beds whenever the orderly
cheerfully called out that it was time for fun and wholesome
sports outdoors. To show us how he covered center field while
the orderly, who pitched for both teams, struck out all the
opposing batters no matter how slowly he lobbed the ball (drugs
and personal distress having cost them their coordination), Kent
put on his baseball cap and sat on the floor with his eyes closed
and his arms hugging his knees.

Gordon giggled. He patted the blanket on each side of his
body, coaxing Jean and me to sit beside him. "I'm a baker, I work
for Wonder Bread," he said, as soon as we joined him; and he
grasped my hand with one of his and Jean's with the other. "I live
in the same house I was born in, with my mother."

"Your mother is dead, Gordon," Kent said mildly, and to Jean
and me he explained that he and Gordon had been made room-
mates because they both had lost people they loved, and were
supposed to help each other meet that truth. What Gordon was
to remind him, in case he forgot, was that he, Kent, had discov-

ered the body of Margaret on her kitchen floor—that she had died of an embolism while preparing the dinner for which he had brought the wine. Kent said those words so bravely that my eyes became damp.

"It was my father who died," Gordon said, and then glanced apprehensively at Kent. "I mean, it was my father who died *first*. . . . It was when I was very young, I don't know just when; but it was because he died that my mother became a Wonder baker, and they gave me her job after her hip went bad and she had to use one of those metal walkers. I have to leave home at 4 A.M. to get to work on time, but my mother says she has to get up to cook my breakfast, so I always set the alarm for 3 A.M. to help her get dressed and to make sure her bathrobe sleeve doesn't catch fire—that happened once—from the burner. In the evenings, we play double solitaire or honeymoon bridge or checkers—"

"Use the past tense, Gordon," Kent said.

"—and listen*ed* to the radio," Gordon said, pronouncing the last two letters as a stressed syllable while looking at Kent with triumph. He chattered on to Jean and me, mainly about his childhood and his mother, but never was too involved with his memories to lack concern for us. I've heard it said that babies will cry at the distress of another small child, as if the world's sufferings were their own; in much the same way, Gordon couldn't control his sobbing when, in response to a question of his, Jean told him that her mother had become an invalid, too, following a stroke, and that her father cared for her until her death from a second stroke. As we finally rose to leave, Gordon said, "Please don't go," but Kent told him gently that we had to, that the visiting hours were over and that it was time for the two of them to rest before going outdoors for their daily innings of wholesome baseball fun. Still, we had to extricate our hands from Gordon's grip before we could rise from the bed. He gave us more cookies at the door, and put his arm on Kent's shoulder. "When will you come back?" he asked, as if nothing in this world mattered more to him. "Tomorrow?"

"As soon as we can," I said.

Walking with Jean under a cloudless sky to the parking lot, I saw, near a small tree, a rose bush in blossom, and thought, "How rich life is!" a response to the sufferings of others that immediately astonished me with its egoism. It was the kind of feeling I sometimes still have upon leaving a tragic play: a sense of the depth of emotion that invests life with its affirmative and yet terrible meaning, combined with relief that I have been nothing but a spectator. In 1956, I was youngish, roughly the age of both Kent and Gordon; unlike them, though, I knew only in an abstract sense what it meant to lose somebody who is deeply loved. My past life seemed but a preparation for my future. I was experiencing the freedom that comes in the interval between jobs, while being elated at the promise of my new position.

* * *

Three decades have elapsed since that June day. I now teach only in the spring terms, having elected to be on what is termed "phased retirement"; my employment line has already been transferred to a younger person on the Cornell creative writing staff. As I have aged, my emotional responses to the knowledge of mortality—my own, that of those I love, family members and close friends; for that matter, that of the civilization of which we all are a part—have continued to surprise me.

Last year, during one of my rare fall-term visits to the campus, I exchanged greetings in a corridor with a Far Eastern specialist who has translated various Japanese texts. I told her about a card an acquaintance of mine and his wife had received, upon the return home of a Japanese couple who had been at Cornell for a number of months. Since neither of the Japanese pair knew much English and both were bewildered by the complexities of establishing a domestic life in a strange country, my friend and his wife had shepherded them about in their search for an apartment, bed linen, kitchen utensils, and an initial supply of food. The card, no doubt purchased in this country just before the couple's departure, contained an engraved message that must have seemed apt to them: "Your thoughtfulness in our hour of deepest need will always be appreciated."

Having a knack for clever rejoinders, the Far Eastern specialist promptly gave me a related example of language misusage—one in which the underlying reference was, if not to death, at least to the keeping of life against the indisputable fact of our human mortality. She told me about the complimentary close of a letter, apparently written with the help of a dual-language dictionary, that somebody she knew had received from an acquaintance in Poland: "May God love and pickle you."

I laughed at her illustration not only because it had outdone mine, but because I had just been freed (my most recent surprise) from a trap of my own devising, and was particularly responsive to anything that treated with humor matters I had been taking too seriously for my own good.

Mortality is a grim condition only if we make it so.

* * *

After six years of living on one of the busiest streets in Ithaca (and not long after the birth of our third son), Jean and I bought a rambling old house at a crossroads in a remote region of our

Finger Lakes county. I had just been granted tenure, that juncture in a professor's life at which the choice of real estate reveals as much about his or her sensibility and expectations as does any list of publications or topics of planned work.

Though the only book I had then published was a critical study of the English writer E. M. Forster, I had written some fiction, including an unsuccessful novel that imitated the comedy of an early novel of his. Disliking the use of the first person, I had nevertheless begun to write in that mode, and out of my own experiences, several years before determining to move to the country. One decision had intimate connections with the other, in that both were responses to a world that suddenly had altered, and not only in my own, and hence possibly idiosyncratic, apprehension of it. For the nuclear bomb, first used against another country by the United States to end the war in which I had been a soldier, now was being manufactured and tested by a third nation that might use it against us. If so, we would retaliate if we could; and that would be the end to everything that counted for much on our little planet. This cheerless prospect produced an intensified, widespread awareness of all the other horrors, including genocide, of which our species is capable, and reverberated beyond Freud's disquieting investigations into the nature of the human unconscious as far back, at least, as the discoveries by Darwin that had prepared the scientific climate for them. We have lived so long with such distrust in ourselves (particularly as nations) that to mention what, around 1960, came as a revelatory shock is to commit a banality.

But such a present-day banality caused several of my colleagues to take their lives, in 1960 and the surrounding years. One of them, a scholar I admired for his kindliness as well as for his humane texts on the American transcendentalists, chose to inhale the exhaust of his idling automobile engine in his closed garage. Next to his body on the car seat there lay the magazine I had given him the previous day for its article on the political gamesmanship underlying the Kennedy espousal of bomb shelters for American families.

Though anything but suicidal, my own response, as a writer, to the new knowledge surprised me: I had suddenly lost the ability or conviction necessary for the composition of third-person fiction. I began to write in the first person only, restricted to what I personally felt to be true, using memory to connect the present moment with the past; for I found that the attempt to construct people separate from myself made them subject to a social reality in which I could find no faith and to an intuited future over which they had no control and which somehow made them not people but lemmings marching (beyond whatever end I gave to their stories) toward a high cliff and an ensuing plunge into dark and icy waters. Conventional fiction (at least that composed on my own typewriter) struck me as a threat, in league with the forces leading to death. And yet the destiny I feared gave me an extraordinary infusion of love for my own family, for all individuals I had come to know and respect, and even for the tiniest creature or object in the natural world. I moved with my family to a country home because I wanted to separate my domestic life from the public and political world as fully as I could, while also desiring, like one of Forster's protagonists, to find meaning for myself and my family through a beloved place and the continuity it would provide with the past.

During the first spring in our Greek Revival farmhouse, Jean and I built a stepping-stone path through the mud between the woodshed door and the cow barn. Like the house, the barn was then more than a hundred thirty years old. Ours was the first non-farming family to occupy the property; while hauling stones for the path from the mounds of them at the edges of the fields (those cairns undoubtedly made as the land was being cleared), I thought it odd that none of our predecessors, who had to slog from house to barn for the morning and night milkings seven days a week, had bothered to build a stone path. I supposed that attention to cows and crops kept these farmers too busy to be concerned about mud.

In our case, it wasn't cows, but the lack of them, that created the need for a decent path. As I could tell from the size of the cistern beneath the porch and the three dug wells, water had been a serious problem on this farm. When the emphasis on rural electrification during the Roosevelt years finally made deep wells with their submersible pumps possible in this far corner of Tompkins County, one had been drilled between the house and the barn. It was the well that now supplied the house, but it says something about the priorities of a Depression-era dairyman that the water was for his herd and not his family. He had installed the pressure tank in the barn, and the warmth of thirty cows kept it from freezing. Without such a symbiotic relationship between water and the users of it, we were constantly turning on taps that gurgled and spat out only a drop or two. A heat tape on the supply pipe was inadequate. So were the Fiberglas insulation and bales of hay I placed around the tank; besides, they caused a heavy condensation that corroded the pressure switch. Even with the arrival of warmer weather, I had to trek back and forth to the barn morning and night to see if we were really out of water or whether I simply needed to push the restart button a half-dozen times while tapping on the switch case with a hammer.

Like many another couple with the dream of a rural sanctuary,

Jean and I had spent all our money on a down payment for a farmhouse with lovely architectural lines; lacking the resources to hire a plumber to move the pressure tank to the basement, we decided to make the necessary trips to the barn as agreeable as possible through that series of little stone islands above the muck.

The task of laying the stones was less pleasurable than we had anticipated, for our pickaxes constantly hit large rocks three to six inches beneath the surface. Some of them we managed to pry up with an old drive shaft I found in the barn; they were smooth and flat as flagstones, and we used them in preference to the ones I had collected. Many of them, though, were too large to pry loose. Not wanting our path to wander around these hidden obstacles, we either found thin stones to place upon them or hauled dirt in the wheelbarrow to raise the ground high enough to bury the thicker ones. An obsessive determination to accomplish a goal can make the mind as rigid as the route it has planned. Only as we were struggling with our final stone did it occur to us that we probably had constructed our walk on top of another, now sunk from sight, that had been built by unknown predecessors—a conjecture whose rightness we immediately proved by probing deep with a pickaxe a foot or so on either side of our new pathway. We collapsed into laughter on the grass, the job having taken so long to complete on weekends that we were now well into the dry season.

Our work, then, lay in intimate contact with that of the dead—perhaps of the husband and wife who in 1831 had supervised the construction of the house (built by a carpenter, according to the information passed on to each new owner by the last one, "for fifty dollars and all the hard cider he could drink") and its assorted barns, the wood for which had come from the immense white pines the first farmer had cleared for his crop lands and pastures. I hadn't expected such a physical confirmation of a spiritual desire for linkage with the past. That confirmation both permitted and made credible my fancy to be buried in the old apple orchard behind the acre of grass, wild strawberries, chicory, and Indian paintbrush that constituted our backyard, and where I would be joined by those I loved, and the generations yet unborn.

*   *   *

In those days, any money I made from writing was so unusual, so removed from the calculations of the household budget, that I considered it mine, to use for any indulgent purpose; and so I appropriated a small royalty windfall to buy two horses, an old farm tractor with a plow and a cutter bar, a hay wagon, and a rusty manure spreader. The pair of horses cost four hundred dollars—with saddles, a supply of metal posts, a large roll of wire, and a fence charger thrown in. Through my labor, our own land would produce all the hay the horses needed. By such means, I hoped further to consolidate my sense of belonging to a farmhouse and its surrounding land.

The decades passed. The world endured, seemingly unchanged, whatever the limited wars and global anxieties of any given moment; but the passage of the years brought death to the other members of the family I had been born into—first to my father, Clayton, through pancreatic cancer, in Ohio; then to my older brother and only sibling, Jack, killed in an automobile accident at the entrance to O'Hare Airport near Chicago; and finally to my very old mother, Grace, who simply stopped breathing as she lay on her bed in our country house, where she had been living for ten years.

On the day after my father's death, my brother and I visited our parents' attorney, a man I had known for years (as a high school student I had done yard work for him) and who now was gray-haired and near retirement, one of those elderly small-town lawyers whose advice and sympathy at times of bereavement complement those of clergymen. "Now, I understand what you are undergoing," this lawyer said to Jack and me, as we were standing in the vestibule of his old house, a Greek Revival much like my own, waiting for him to lead us into his office for a discussion of my father's estate, with its pitifully few belongings. "You are both aware, in a way that is new to you, that your own days are numbered."

Clichés, those long-dulled expressions of general truths about others, can become scalpels when used against us and our secret truths. My memory of these words is no doubt altered by my present awareness that Jack's days were to be more severely numbered than my own; but I believe that I hold the actual moment clearly enough in mind to re-experience the bond between my brother and me at that instant, as we looked at each other, knowing from the expression of embarrassment on the other's face that both of us were guilty of thinking of ourselves at a moment when we should be experiencing nothing but grief for a dead father and concern for a surviving mother and wife.

"No, you needn't feel any shame, it's natural," the lawyer went on, putting one arm on my brother's shoulder and the other on mine. "I responded the same way, and so does every son. Maybe it takes the shock of death for a son to realize that he has always identified himself with his father, and I suppose the same goes for a daughter and her mother. If you're like the rest of us, you haven't seen until this moment the necessity of making your wills."

As a veteran teacher of creative writing courses, one who has read many autobiographical accounts thinly disguised as fiction, I have come to know much about the hidden resentments and open antagonisms between children and their parents. At graduation time, during the receptions my college holds for the graduates and their families, I have often been touched not only by the affinity in bone structure that connects a particular son with the father with whom he seems to have spent his adolescence battling, but by an almost uncanny resemblance in gesture—a shy or defiant way of brushing back the hair, say—and in the timbre and mannerisms of speech.

During my first sabbatical leave, spent with my wife and children in Paris, I saw my father's face within my own, one day while I was shaving; perhaps because I was so far from America, perhaps because of a certain loneliness for home, I found myself not only accepting, but welcoming, the genetic bond I saw in the mirror, and I suppose I remember that moment because my response was so unexpected. For, throughout most of my adult life, up to my father's final months, I had tried to find my identity in opposition to what I took to be his, and only as he was dying was I released from my separate conception of myself; and now that Clayton was dead, as the old lawyer had said, I had been jolted into a new knowledge of the brevity of my own life.

Whatever the interpretation Freud gave to a Greek myth from his own observations and experiences within a particular epoch and its culture, I find it likely, from my own, that patricide is more the transformation of a suicidal impulse than the result of sexual rivalry over a wife and a mother; at least, as best as I can imagine such a wild and uncontrollable disturbance, the son who would kill his father must be embittered by his own human condition, and be flailing to free himself from a biological entrapment that goes back through the ages.

*   *   *

My brother's death came so suddenly that it took me some days to accept it, a lack of comprehension that I shared (though with less psychological reason) with my mother, who then was in her nineties and already living with Jean and me. On the other hand, I had expected my mother's death, which came shortly after our celebration of her hundredth birthday. I had always felt myself to be close to her, especially in my childhood and in her final years, during which she had kept her wit and love for me and my family and had not permitted herself to fret over her declining strength. I worried during her last years about the effect her dying would have upon me; I understood Gordon as I had been unable to more than a quarter of a century earlier, and knew myself more fortunate than he—not only because my mother had lived so much longer than had his, but because I had a wife and children to love, and to be a support for me.

From Grace, who had met her own death without fear, I learned how much more terrible it is to lose a husband and then a son than it is to give up one's own life. If this was something I had previously known, I knew it so intimately from my mother's death that I considered it a truth I would never forget. Indeed, that knowledge made me so impatient with those poets who, having reached thirty, feel obligated to write self-centered poems about their mortality that once, in the midst of a lecture about a poem like that, I told an auditorium of undergraduates that only the young worry about their dying. The older you get, I said, the more you realize that nothing matters so much as the continued existence of those whom you love—and I said all this so persuasively, with such inner conviction, that the auditorium was filled with the kind of silence we sometimes hear when hundreds of minds are conjoined, as if telepathically, through a single voice.

* * *

How is it that we can continue to know something as a truth, perhaps the major truth of our stay on Earth, and still have part of our minds suddenly reject it? In the years immediately following my sixtieth birthday, I began to worry, without good cause, about dying, and to speculate as to what I would do if—like my father and his father before him; like, for that matter, my mother's brother and maybe those other, more distant, members on both sides of my family who had died of lengthy and undiagnosed ailments—I developed cancer.

On the day I visited Kent in the mental hospital, my own life, as I have said, stretched before me, full of promise. I suppose that, upon reaching sixty, I felt I had achieved whatever had been promised, and was looking back more than forward, and maybe wishing my talents had given me more than they apparently were capable of offering. Also, I had been presenting any number of eulogies at memorial services for older colleagues, as well as for lifelong friends—including one for Kent, whom Jean and I had loved enough to consider a member of our family.

His mental equilibrium had remained perilous, sustained by psychiatric treatment as well as by the depth of his caring for others, while being disrupted by the deaths of close acquaintances and the general violence and injustices of the world beyond—something his generation and mine might be particularly susceptible to, having absorbed in childhood from a more innocent America a belief in the stability and inherent goodness of things. But it was a heart attack that sent him to the hospital, where a second attack brought his death.

Kent had been a lexicographer for more than thirty years. At the memorial service, a colleague spoke of him as born to the craft, with a sensitivity to language, an inherent taste and style, and a sense of humor—an attribute necessary for a profession defined by Samuel Johnson, a lexicographer himself, as "harmless drudgery." The colleague mentioned that Kent's favorite dictionary definition was the one for *corncob*. Though it had preceded his tenure on the staff, Kent had jealously guarded the rhythm and resonant sounds of that humble object's definition ("The woody core of an ear of corn, on which the kernels grow in rows") through revision after revision of the dictionary. In my eulogy, I tried to explain those qualities of Kent's that contributed to my sense of the richness of life, as I had left him in the mental hospital in 1956.

Driving back to Ithaca from the service, Jean and I laughed at the story of Kent's preservation of a definition, but I found myself wondering how long *corncob* would be so defined, and how long dictionaries and their attempts at precision would matter, in a world that, in its rush toward Armageddon (a term that now and again found its way into our present American leader's public utterances), daily mangled not only the meanings of words but humans and their meaning. How much easier it would be to accept the biological fact that all lives, including our own, have an end if the future of the race promised betterment of our moral nature, if there was a genuine prospect of world peace for our descendants! A proposal like the recent one for a Strategic Defense Initiative ("Star Wars"), which increased the threat of what ostensibly it would avert, seemed to bear out the disturbing possibility that I first heard proposed during a 1960

lecture by a celebrated prophet of our culture—that as a fatigued
and elderly civilization aware of a void where once it had found
spiritual essence, we actually might be *willing* the blossoming
sarcoma of the bomb. Such a conjecture is itself malignant, one
we must oppose with all our might. And yet Kent's death from
other causes increased my fear of dying from cancer, as if it were
an inevitable scourge.

It was not I but one of my sons who, late in the spring of 1985,
developed the disease. Luckily, it was the form most amenable to
treatment, through surgery and radiation; his cancer is not in
remission, but apparently gone, burned out from the lymph
system—though, to make sure, he will require annual checkups
for several more years.

I was sitting alone at the picnic table in our enclosed side
porch, eating a sandwich (on sunny days, I used to escort my
mother to that porch, so that we could eat lunch there, while
together turning the puffy white clouds we saw above the distant ridge of Connecticut Hill into an imagined bestiary and
watching the occasional hummingbird poised just beyond the
screen or glass) on the day that my son returned from a visit to
his doctor, to say almost jauntily, "Well, I guess I've got some
bad news."

Jean and I sat for three hours in the surgery waiting room of
Tompkins Community Hospital, while our son's spleen was
removed and biopsies taken from other parts of the lymph
system and nearby organs—an operation whose outcome, we
were told, could be considered especially favorable if it turned
out to be unnecessary, the spleen having been discovered to be
unaffected and no further tumors found. According to those
terms, the operation was a complete success.

To regain his strength for the radiation therapy that again

would sap it, our son took brief walks, then longer ones, and finally was jogging the four miles that constitute a country block in our region, or riding his bicycle the five miles to Connecticut Hill and then along the dirt roads and trails of the forested spine—a land-use area—that he loved. In the evenings, waiting for his return, Jean and I had philosophical discussions about death, and the immense value it imparts to life. To realize that sooner or later every stranger you pass on the street is to die makes that person no longer separate from you. It seemed to us impossible that anybody possessed of enough imagination to know what death meant, either to himself or to another, could possibly lust for power over others, or could torture or kill a victim, or could desire to annihilate a competing power, a different people.

For his radiation therapy, our son had to drive daily to the Upstate Medical Center in Syracuse. Since the treatments sometimes made him feel weak or doubtful of the quickness of his responses, I usually accompanied him, to share in the task of driving. The trip from and back to our house covered almost a hundred fifty miles, all of them through the gentle hills of the Finger Lakes countryside, the portion near Syracuse along a crest of a wide and fecund valley created in the last glacial age. The days of that summer were unusually sunny and mild, and the visibility was sharp. Soon we were bringing along a pair of binoculars, so that the passenger could look at whatever in the distance took his fancy—a bird, a farmhouse on a slope, a dirt road winding up through a gap in the opposing crest and bordering a creek. On the return trip, if the treatment that day had not taken away my son's appetite, we would stop at a restaurant in a village not far from Syracuse, for the chef there made particularly appetizing soups; and while we ate, we would look at a detailed regional map, in order to find yet another route, however circuitous, back to our home—a route that would enable us, maybe, to pass a particular pond or one of the smaller of the Finger Lakes we'd never seen, or to find a dirt road that might lead to a glorious hilltop vista. Hidden by a buttoned and long-sleeved shirt were the indelible marks on my son's skin that outlined for the technician the area for the X-ray treatments; a baseball cap covered the new baldness at the back of his scalp.

Given the nature of our daily mission, why did those trips give me happiness? If happiness is not to be distinguished from hope, something we both had, it is to be sharply distinguished from an absorption in the self that makes a person perceive himself as a likely victim of his genes and of his century's ills. Even before my son had finished his sentence about bad news on the day I was eating my sandwich on the porch, I knew what he was about to reveal, and already was attempting, by an act of will that precluded any possibility of victimization, to transfer the nasty stuff spreading in his body to my own.

Despite the worry and the daily trips to Syracuse, I discovered myself quickly writing a comic novel (this time, one without a debt to Forster) about events on another planet, events that covered nearly everything that had distressed me about our own world for the past quarter century. Apparently the creative restriction I had felt since 1960 had vanished: if I was all of the characters I dreamed up, I was also none of them.

Meanwhile, I began to develop mysterious symptoms, and they continued long after my son's radiation treatments had been concluded. I developed rashes, facial swellings, throat obstructions (my grandfather had died of throat cancer), pains in the area of the pancreas (though my father had felt none), and spells of vertigo. Briefly, my blood showed an alarming decrease in white cells, a sure sign to me that my own lymph system had gone awry. While waiting for a promised letter from my doctor containing information about my latest blood test (why would he have written instead of phoning, unless the news was grim?), a letter which for five days was lost in the mail, I wrote on, chuckling as I went, for twelve to fourteen hours at a stretch, simply wanting to get the book finished before I died.

It is possible that some of my symptoms were the result of methanol or some other poison in the cheap imported wine I was drinking. The mind is a mighty instrument, capable of feats as miraculous as they are mad, but I doubt that mine was capable of affecting the nature of my blood. Still, all signs of disease vanished from my body at the time of my son's first checkup, six months after the therapy had been concluded, the thorough examination that showed *his* body to be free of cancer. However irrational my attempt to wrest a disease from my son by making it my own, the strength of my desire to do so has freed me forever, I would guess, from a consuming dread of it or any other possibly mortal ailment.

*   *   *

Having brought this chronicle of surprises up to the latest to occur, I sit at my desk in a large and (except for me and assorted cats and dogs) empty house, for both my son and wife are at Cornell, one a student older than most, his recent illness having determined him to prepare for a new career, and the other a long-time employee. As I look through a window at the snow from our first November storm now gleaming in the sunlight on the backyard and on the branches of the trees beyond it, I realize, from the very fact that I felt it necessary to write this account, that I have not really been liberated from myself, or from the reasons that brought me to autobiographical prose of this sort, and probably never shall, even were perpetual world peace and the brotherhood and sisterhood of humanity to be pealed from every church bell tomorrow morning; for I contain within myself everything I have ever thought, every fear or pleasure I have ever experienced, whatever the stages I have passed through. And, in my opinion, for a brief span each of us is the still-living civilization itself, a microcosm of its past as well as its present—and so each of us is capable of responding with all of the old immediacy to the eighteenth-century rose bush we can no longer draw in the former way, to the Romantic symphony we can no longer compose, as well as to the subjective terrors and countless acts of bigotry and cruelty and large-scale violence that have marked our passage.

The trees beyond the yard constitute a young walnut grove that on its own accord (but with the help of squirrels) has replaced the old apple orchard where once I wanted to be buried. I see what is, but know what was, and again can feel that impulse to be part of this land, however much I recognize that neither I nor my wife nor my children can possibly rest beneath the blossoming apple boughs that, through the agency of a stepping-stone path, gave me this fancy, nor anywhere else on ground whose ownership only temporarily has been vested in us.

Half the stones that Jean and I planted upon those of others have already disappeared beneath the earth, and the remaining ones have settled far enough into the turf to become separate stone-bottomed pools whenever it rains. For some years, we've had a new and apparently inexhaustible supply of well water, and the pressure tank has been moved from barn to basement; for that matter, the old cow barn was destroyed in a fire decades ago, to be replaced by a horse stable that I built with the help of my sons and wife.

But I continue to walk the path morning and night, to feed and stroke and speak to Smoky, our elderly remaining horse, whose affection I would win back. For Smoky's attitude toward me has subtly changed, ever since his recent discovery that I was incapable of saving the life of the thirty-year-old mare, Tammy, his beloved stablemate. She died, as horses her age frequently do—so the veterinarian who tended her told me—of a visceral cancer. Maybe what Smoky chiefly resents is that I was an accomplice in the difficult removal of Tammy's half-ton body from the stable, helping the man from the rendering works who had been recommended to me by the vet; in any event, Smoky no longer whinnies at my approach, and won't even look directly at me.

Horses have fine memories—in some ways, more remarkable than ours—but often they don't know how to use the past intelligently, in my opinion. For them, a frightening discovery or untoward occurrence remains isolated from all other events, never becoming simply an integral part of a larger and more forgiving context or world picture. "May God bless and pickle you, Smoky, you old fart," I sometimes tell him, vexed that he won't nuzzle my jacket pocket for whatever surprise—a carrot or dried ear of corn—I may have for him. Still, it just may be that tonight Smoky will be as glad to see me as I will be to see my wife and son returning together from their day at Cornell. It is also an opinion of mine that *tonight* is as far into the future as one's hopes or worries reasonably ought to go.

1988

⌒Skiing
at Hector

ACOUPLE OF Sundays ago, my wife, Jean, and I went skiing
at Hector. That name, while no longer technically correct
even as shorthand, is the abbreviation for "Hector Land
Use Area" by which residents in the surrounding area refer,
through long custom, to a ridge equidistant between the two
largest of the Finger Lakes, Seneca and Cayuga. Like the Connecticut Hill area, a state-managed preserve whose ridge I can
see from the south windows of our old country house, Hector
(which I can see from the windows to the west) is composed of
land whose topsoil long ago proved too thin and infertile for
continued farming. Both preserves are used for hunting, skiing,
hiking, picnicking, and camping; both contain a number of
ponds, most of them man-made, for the deer, birds, and other
wildlife.

Unlike Connecticut Hill, Hector belongs to the federal government, and the area is the more tamed of the two. As a

convenience to equestrians, the rangers long ago built a split-rail paddock, and marked some of the trails for horseback riders as well as hikers and skiers. Over the years they have kept a number of the larger fields once used for farming free of brush and saplings through annual mowing, which not only makes a portion of the area look like a well-groomed park but provides for marvelous vistas, particularly at sunset, of the far shore of Seneca Lake. These fields have a practical as well as an aesthetic function: in summer and fall they serve as common land for nearby farmers who bring their cattle there, to graze. In late fall, these farmers have a roundup, riding horseback like western cowboys as they drive the livestock into holding pens, there to identify them by ear tag before hauling them back to their respective farms. The roundup always attracts many spectators.

A few years back, the federal government, as a means of combating debt, declared its intention to put land-use areas like Hector up for sale. The local outcry, though, was so pained and intense that it became an embarrassment to regional Republican politicians, associated as they were with the administration in Washington, and an asset to Democrats desiring their offices. To protect the land in perpetuity, Congress, at the last moment and no doubt as a rider to some more important bill, designated Hector as the Finger Lakes National Forest—certainly one of the tiniest of such forests in the public domain. I suppose the awareness of how close this bit of loveliness once was to extinction through subdivision has made it more precious than ever, and by its traditional name. I would never say to my wife, "Would you like to go skiing in the Finger Lakes National Forest?" On Saturday and Sunday alike, I asked her if she would like to ski at Hector.

Saturday would have been preferable, being one of those

winter days that can make the season not only exhilarating but seemingly as open and free as summer. The sunlight sparkled on fresh snow, the temperature held at twenty, the wind was calm. But Jean said she was feeling a little queasy, and wasn't sure she was up to skiing; and I said I had a lot to do anyway, and probably shouldn't afford the time.

Both Jean and I are in our mid-sixties. The previous winter, neither of us had skied at all, not so much because we felt too old for it but because Jean was still recovering from a knee fracture; summer before last, she took an awkward fall while climbing over a pile of lumber by the barn in the attempt to see if the wild raspberries were ripe. One of her bones was crushed. Her surgeon had to graft some bone from her hip as a replacement, using a couple of screws to hold things together. It's possible that what made her feel queasy on Saturday was the thought of what might happen, if she fell while skiing; her knee, while mended, won't bend as much as it used to.

I don't suppose I would have suggested skiing if Saturday hadn't been so fine and if she hadn't enjoyed so much an Adirondack canoeing trip in late summer. Two of our sons live in New York City, but the third, Cris, works for a honey processing firm in Newfield, just over Connecticut Hill from our house, and so continues to live at home; he accompanied Jean and me on that canoeing trip. We explored the Osgood River for several days, camping along the shore, and later canoed on Middle Saranac Lake and along the Saranac River. While we were still at our Osgood site, Cris, while consulting that venerable book known to Adirondack canoeing enthusiasts simply as "Jamieson"—Paul Jamieson's *Adirondack Canoe Waters: North Flow*—came across a reference to a side trip for Osgood River canoeists, a bushwhacking climb up Star Mountain, whose top provides a good vista. "Topo map and compass," says Jamieson, "are essential." Cris coaxed Jean into the attempt, pointing out the relative smallness of the mountain, and saying that if the climb became difficult for her, we'd turn back. Using the compass, Cris led us precisely to the indicated vista, Jean managing to get over or around fallen trees and rocks with not much more difficulty than I; at the top we had lunch. I took the compass for the downward trip, guiding us to within a few feet of our beached canoe. All of us were delighted with ourselves. Of course, on that bushwhacking trip there weren't many hazards, other than getting lost in the forest; the ground was as firm as it was dry, and nobody had to worry about a bad fall. Afterwards, Jean said that the rigorous exercise had been good for her knee.

The work that I used as my excuse for not going skiing on Saturday was mostly mental, and dealt less with research for a project I had in mind than with whether or not we should make an appointment with a nearby vet to have our dog, Puppsy-Daisy, killed. For rural people, the euphemism for having an animal killed is "to have her put down," even as, for city people, it is "to have her put to sleep." Veterinarians use the word "euthanasia"; sometimes, lacking a handy and innocuous verb, they turn that noun into one, making a fatal injection sound like the polishing of a car. Over the years, I have trained myself to avoid evasions like that, in order, I say, to face up to the seriousness of the act. In recent months, though, I have begun to suspect my reason to be a more hypocritical one—to prevent me from ever having it done, however merciful and just the decision.

A faithful mongrel ever since she had come begging at the back door for admission into our lives fifteen years ago, Puppsy-Daisy had outlived by several years the two puppies that we already owned. She had been too feeble and full of shivers the previous winter to be left in the unheated woodshed attached to the house, despite the soft bed of cedar chips we had provided, and had become too incontinent to be permitted inside. So that we could heat the enclosed side porch night and day for her by leaving the door to the house open except for a folding gate, Jean and I had spent an extravagant sum on insulating quilts (the sort that, tightly held by channels to the window frame, can be raised and lowered like shades) for each of the five sliding Thermopanes. Over the following summer, Puppsy-Daisy gradually became deaf and blind, and this winter seemed to be losing even her sense of smell: sometimes I had to tap the bowl against her nose, to let her know her food was ready. Still, she showed no suffering, and ate with as much greedy pleasure as ever, and wagged her tail whenever anybody stroked her. But what kind of existence were we subjecting her to, by giving her a daily senior dog-citizen capsule so she'd have enough energy, once we raised her to her feet, to be guided into the frozen outdoors three or four times a day? Jean and I long ago told each other that we wanted no life-sustaining efforts made on our behalf, were we to find ourselves deprived of will and many of our other faculties. Did we really mean what we said, though, if we were unable to end the life of a household pet of such decrepitude? All Saturday I was too indecisive to call the vet.

* * *

On Sunday, Cris woke us to say that if we wanted to ski we should go in the morning, because the day was turning unseasonably warm and rain was expected by late afternoon. He had been skiing all Saturday with friends, and was going with another group that morning, but had too much good sense to ask us to join them. A true cross-country skier, Cris finds his way through terrain that strikes me as inaccessible, using the same aids—compass and topographical map—that we depended upon for bushwhacking the previous summer. Sometimes he starts from the top of Connecticut Hill and travels down the slopes and far into the neighboring county, even crossing the ice of Cayuta, one of the smaller lakes.

When I asked Jean if she felt good enough to ski a bit this day, she said we both probably would have felt better on Saturday if we had, and that we might be sorry if we put it off any longer. The day was cloudy and windy; by the time we finished a leisurely breakfast with the Sunday *New York Times*, the temperature had risen to forty. When it's on top of an icy base, melting snow makes for a particularly slippery surface. We dabbed red klister, a sticky substance with the consistency of toothpaste, on the middle part of our skis, and took off for Hector. I suggested we try the easiest route I knew of, the two-mile section of the Interlochen trail running through the woods between the Blueberry Patch Campground and Foster Pond.

"Do you remember the place where we always used to fall, to avoid hitting the tree at the bend just beyond the slope?" I asked Jean. She remembered, but wasn't sure she would recognize the hazard before she was already picking up speed on that slope, so I said I would take the lead. We put on our skis on opposite sides of the tree at the beginning of the trail. She was planning, of course, to follow me; but her skis were so slippery—not enough red klister—that she sailed on ahead, while I—too much klister—was glued to the snow. Off balance, she held to a branch for support, waiting for me to clump up to her side. Luckily, she had brought the tube of red klister, and added more to her skis while I scraped off as much as I could from mine.

Though we have skied cross-country for years, we'd never

paid much attention to technique, being content to step aside to let all those crouching others, poles deftly tucked under elbows, zoom past us down the steeper hills; being content, too (in those winters before her fracture), to take an undignified tumble whenever conditions were beyond our control. On Sunday, though, we both felt as awkward and graceless as we had on the day we first went skiing. The snow not only was slippery, but melting away so fast that tree roots already had emerged, ready to catch our ski tips. And there were dogs, frisky as Puppsy-Daisy used to be. A Dalmatian and a mostly St. Bernard galloped around a bend. Frantic with friendliness, they nearly knocked me to the ground with their leaps and muzzle nudges. When their owner, a young woman, came around the curve, she just missed a collision both with me and her dogs; she wasn't much of a skier on such a surface, either. "Come on, fellows," she said casually to them, but had such difficulty getting started that they were out of sight before she began to move.

"This is the dangerous spot," I warned Jean, a little farther down the trail. Both of us got off the tracks, to find a safer way to descend; but it wasn't the spot, after all. I warned her two more times of the approaching hazard before I actually found myself sailing down it, to topple in the snow to avoid the tree by the bend. Jean took off her skis. Later, as she was making a turn on an almost level portion of the trail, going at a fair speed, she did lose her balance and fall, right on the bad knee. She lay in the snow for a few minutes, rubbing the knee—but smiling, to let me know nothing much had gone wrong; and then she got to her feet as readily as if she were twenty years younger. "Good for you," I cried, exultant for her sake.

It is always the case that the skiers one passes on the trails at Hector smile or give a nod, glad to acknowledge their comradeship, for this one moment of time, with a stranger, and sometimes to hand on information about the trail ahead; one young man said cheerfully to me, "You're five minutes from the pond," though it took Jean and me ten before we arrived. At the top of the last small rise before reaching the pond, we came upon a group of six men and women in their late thirties who were poised before the downgrade, laughing at the hesitancy of two in their party. They were travelling the length of the Interlochen trail, they said, with a car at either end; in the car at the Blueberry Patch Campground parking lot, a pot of chili was waiting, to be heated on their camp stove, if ever they arrived. We skied on, up to the sign that said "Foster Pond." The pond itself, covered with snow and ice, seemed simply a flat part of the landscape; but since it had been our goal, we stayed by the sign for a time before starting back.

On the return trip, we didn't worry about slippery slopes and hazardous trees. We felt like pretty good skiers. Cross-country skiing is the winter equivalent of canoeing. Both activities propel you almost silently through a natural landscape; some of the evergreens you pass on a curving ski trail might well be the trees lining the meanders of a narrow stream like the Osgood River, and in both cases you have to duck now and then under the generous boughs. As the sun emerged from a cloud, I felt the return of a happiness I had known on the canoeing trip the previous summer.

Our canoe had been heavily loaded with three passengers and all our camping gear for the trip across Middle Saranac Lake. As it often does there, the wind picked up, driving whitecaps of the sort that, if met broadside, can founder a canoe already low in the water; but Cris, at the stern, was able to keep us generally headed toward the distant island we thought would make a good camping spot, if other canoeists hadn't gotten there first. It turned out to be almost two islands, with a pair of forested hillocks connected by a natural causeway. Not only was it deserted, but the forest service had built a picnic table and a privy, luxuries after our stay in the wilderness of the Osgood River; and, no doubt to prevent the despoilation of the island's fragile environment, had left, next to a handsome grill, a good supply of kindling and cut and seasoned hardwood logs. The wind died, and the sun came out; after we set up camp, we went swimming in Middle Saranac's blue and cool purity, and then lay on the warmth of a rock that sloped into the water, looking at nearby Ampersand Mountain and the other and more distant high peaks while feeling the gentle lapping of the waves on our feet.

That night the sky was lit by lightning, and thunder reverberated against the mountains; the rain pounded our tents, but we remained safe and dry. We had planned to return home the next day. The morning, though, was cloudless, the lake absolutely still, and the atmosphere so clear that it gave all of us the sense of being gifted with new and uncanny sight. Having elected to remain for another day without ever coming to a vote, we decided to paddle leisurely along the lake shore and then downstream on the winding Saranac River.

On the river, we let the current carry us along while we looked at the families of ducks and an occasional blue heron. We stopped off to explore a little glen with its stream, beaver dam, and small pool, walking the paths that bear and deer had made through the ferns. The glen was filled with mushrooms for Cris to look at; he has become an expert at mushroom identification, and is pleased to come across an exotic specimen, whether edible or not. While Cris and Jean wandered about, I sat on a mossy boulder under which the mountain stream gurgled, listening to that sound while watching the dazzle of the sun through the forest canopy, and felt a happiness so complete that the previous day's pleasure seemed only a way of preparing me for it. We stayed in that glen for maybe half an hour, before continuing to drift down the river. When I tried to explain to Jean and Cris how I had felt, they said they had felt that happiness too; Jean said that maybe it was the kind of happiness that is carried in our genes from our primeval ancestors, and has something to do with our heritage in the natural world.

Further down the river, we entered a lock. The tender came out of his cabin to lower our canoe three feet (what an added Adirondack park service luxury, to be given the treatment of a yacht!), and drifted onward to Lower Saranac Lake. The return journey, upstream, was a bit more strenuous, though not difficult, and we renewed our acquaintance with the lock tender, the duck family, and the herons.

In any event, that was the happiness that had come back to me, upon our return along the trail that had taken us as far as Foster Pond on a slushy winter day; and maybe both times it had been partly caused not only by my genes but by pleasure at my Jean's pluckiness, then for climbing a mountain as well as under-going all the normal physical stress of camping and canoeing, and now for coming up smiling from a fall. The day after we came home from that vacation in the Adirondacks, I wrote a letter to a couple who were two of Jean's and my surviving friends from our younger days; though or because the husband had bone cancer, I thought that both of them might like to hear about a kind of happiness that they, as long-time canoeists, probably had experienced themselves, and so told them about the mountain and the island and the glen.

The wife wrote back almost immediately, to say that she had

read to her husband what I had written, that he had smiled, and that she had forwarded the letter to their son in diplomatic service overseas. The son flew home soon afterwards, when his father's condition suddenly worsened, and was with him for his last days. Later, back in Thailand, that son wrote Jean and me a letter about the nature of happiness. He, too, believed it a gift of our distant forebears, and he went on to recount memories from his childhood that were happy ones, and linked our respective families. I was thinking about that correspondence as Jean and I were skiing back to the Blueberry Campground parking lot with what I took to be exceptional speed and grace.

At the parking lot, the group we had met on the trail were standing around a propane stove, waiting for their chili to bubble. They smiled and waved, and so did we; and then Jean and I drove home.

∗   ∗   ∗

Though clearly nothing much had happened during our morning at Hector, Jean and I both were glad we had gone. As we were waiting for our lunch of leftovers to warm in the oven, we sat at the kitchen table, talking about triumphs from our childhood. I said that in the second or third grade I was given a "D" in reading that was a result of my inability to read aloud a pre-selected passage from my primer on the day that parents came to class, to hear their children perform; but that later in the same spring, while undergoing a lengthy convalescence in bed, I read the entirety of Rudyard Kipling's *The Light That Failed*, and that it had made such a profound impression on me that I still remembered not only the sadness it engendered but the view from my partly opened bedroom window of our garage, softly lit as it was by the radiance of a setting sun. Jean said that I had a tendency to exaggerate, but she could believe that I had read an adult novel as, say, a third-grader, since she herself, as a first-grader, had been in an experimental master class in Cleveland that had been reading at sixth-grade level by the end of the year. In the seventh grade, I said, I attended a junior high school in Fort Smith, Arkansas, in which the pupils in every class sat in accordance with their course standing, which was based on weekly tests and other written work. Finding it a bore to remain in the first seat of the first row for every one of my subjects, I would intentionally make errors on several consecutive tests, to see how far back such miscues would put me, and also how quickly I could return to the premier seat. Jean said that as a child she had thought there wasn't a profession in the world at which she couldn't excel, the only problem that worried her being which profession to choose.

We weren't boasting of our respective childhoods because of satisfaction with our skiing expedition so much as we were making an unstated comparison between early promise and what actually had come about, in the ensuing half century and then some. Puffing up our young triumphs like that was a way of acknowledging an acceptance of life, especially of our lives together; and of whatever it was that we had as well as hadn't achieved.

I guess that people can be changed, if just a little, by a brief and uneventful ski trip through the woods. On Monday morning, with Jean's approval, I called the vet—though I admit I didn't say I wanted Puppsy-Daisy killed. I asked the vet to put her down; and Jean, Cris, and I were all there, to stroke her fur and murmur words she couldn't hear, as the fatal needle gently went in.

1990

ᴇ꒰Stories from My Life with the Other Animals

I. AMERICANS IN ITALY

TWO DECADES ago, my wife, Jean, and I and two of our sons—Jimmy, who was nine, and Cris, who was seventeen—spent a year in Italy. We lived in a spacious second-floor apartment in a villa that was surrounded by olive trees, grapevines, and hillside fields but yet was within walking distance of downtown Florence. The owners of the villa—an Italian and his English-born wife—and their children occupied most of the large sixteenth-century stone dwelling. We thought of the wife as our landlady, since she handled the business operations of the house and its land, supervising what, without any self-consciousness at all, she called its "peasants"—the couple who lived in the gate house and maintained the lawns and flower gardens, and the other couple who lived in the *casa colonica*, a farmhouse separated by a patio from the villa itself, and did the agricultural work. It was difficult to tell the age of the farming couple; the husband appeared to be considerably older than his wife, and I first mistook him to be the grandfather of his two young children.

Her many years in Italy had made our landlady, both in gestures and attitude, more Italian—or so it seemed to Jean and me—than many of the lifelong residents of Florence whom we met. When she gave us the key to our apartment, she told us that if police or other city officials paid us a call, we were to tell them that we were "exchange" visitors who paid no rent directly in money but instead were offering our house in the United States to members of her family; for she wished to avoid the municipal tax on our rent. We considered the rent remarkably modest, and were willing to pay more to cover the tax and thus to avoid any possible penalties to her. "Oh, no, no, no," she said, vigorously shaking her head; it was obvious that, unaware of local customs, we were impugning her skill at constructing socially expected stratagems. "The government adds fifteen percent to the regular taxes," she told us. "This is to cover cheating, which, as you can see, is therefore legal, up to a certain point. Occasionally an inspector checks our dustbins, to determine if we have any foreign renters; but he knows as well as I that Maria [she was the woman who lived in the gate house] daily burns the garbage of our renters."

She also told us that one of the villa cats, given the English name of Monster, considered our apartment his home, and would expect us to feed him. In our farmhouse in the Finger Lakes region of upstate New York, dogs and cats (usually several of each species) lived with us, and on winter mornings Jean and I often woke up to find most of them snuggled up next to us; it sometimes seemed to me they had an unfair advantage over our two horses in the unheated barn we had built for them. I felt as much affection for the horses—particularly for the quarter horse, Smoky, whom we had bought when he was a colt small enough to put his head on my shoulder, as he followed me about in the paddock—as I did for the household pets, and in the earlier years of our life in that farmhouse, mature adult though I assumed myself to be, I sometimes wakened on particularly cold mornings to a pleasurable fantasy that put *all* of our animals in bed with Jean and me.

During our year in Italy, our oldest son, Larry, who was a senior at Cornell, had remained at home, living in the farmhouse with other students; he had promised to care for the domestic animals as well as to feed the birds once the snows came. He was a responsible son, and had listened carefully to all my instructions—including my warning to him to fill the bird feeder with seed only around midnight, and to do it as quietly as he could. The reason for such stealth was to prevent Tammy, Smoky's stablemate, from seeing or hearing him at the bird feeder; for if she did, that mare surely would jump the top paddock rail and eat all the seed before setting off down the road. In Florence, I realized how much I missed the chores of animal care that I had sometimes considered irksome, as well as the idiosyncrasies of each of our animals; and so was glad to have a surrogate for at least our cats.

Monster, though, never provided us with much companionship. Despite his name, he was a scrawny little animal; the name was the result of a missing ear, torn fur, scars, and continual fresh wounds. The most severe of these injuries had been inflicted upon him by his worst enemy, a vicious tomcat from the neighboring villa who claimed the territory as his own, the rest of them by the other cats who lived with our landlady and her family in a relationship quite different from the one we had with our animals. Except for the occasions on which these cats were discovered using the shelf above the kitchen cabinets for their personal bathroom and would be chased out of the house for a few minutes, they were treated with the tolerance that is another name for indifference; it was as if they were visited upon the family by a fate its members had to accept as well as they could. In consequence, the cats never to my knowledge asked for affection, never engaged in activities designed to please their owners, never showed off in the manner our cats always have. (For example, Fearless Fosdick, one of our present cats, climbs a backyard tree only while guests are sitting in the lawn chairs beneath it, and continually looks down to note their alarm or consternation as she—Fearless Fosdick is aptly named except for her sex—edges out farther and farther on a limb bending under her weight.)

Perpetually wounded pariah among cats though he might have been, Monster was as indifferent to humans as any other cat on the villa grounds. He spent his days lurking on the roof tiles, coming down only to be fed. As an Italian cat, he spurned milk or the chicken giblets Jean several times cooked for him; he had an appetite only for huge plates of spaghetti, which he preferred with cheese and tomato sauce. Whenever our cats desire milk, they alter their conventional miaow—or so it has always seemed to me—to make it approximate that English word; the only sound that ever came from Monster was a brusque but self-satisfied "ciao" after he finished his plate and headed for the door. Perhaps, in the interval between renters in which he may have scavenged upon the remains of rodents or birds left by the more aggressive cats, he had ingested parasites; in any event, several months into our stay, he began to lose his appetite, and finally died from a massive infestation of worms. (We repeatedly told our landlady that he had stopped eating his spaghetti, but such news led her only to that well-known Italian gesture of helplessness, a shrug accompanied by hands raised palms-up. When at last, observing herself how feeble he was, she rushed him off to a veterinarian in remorse, Monster was too far gone to be saved.)

One shouldn't generalize about the attitudes toward animals of Italians on the basis of a single family, especially a family with an English wife and mother, I know; all that I can say is that this family had a much more casual relationship with their pets than I did. Still, that casual attitude was but a step removed from the callousness of other Italians to animals outside the household, for by and large they seemed to regard them simply as objects for sport or consumption. Though the husband who lived in the farmhouse was pleased, for the sake of his children, to be given the little potted evergreen decorated with miniature lights with which we had celebrated an advance Christmas (we spent the actual holiday in Sicily), he was insensitive enough to kill a rabbit for his family's dinner by thrusting a pointed stick through its eye and into the brain while Jimmy and one of his school friends were admiring all of the rabbits he kept in cages. Apparently it never occurred to him that such a killing, accompanied by a shriek from the rabbit, might be such a psychic shock to an American nine-year-old that he would have nightmares for weeks.

And I was almost equally appalled by the slaughter of song-birds by Italian males who, unlike that peasant, were prosperous enough to afford guns and ammunition. We had taken rooms in the major hotel at Assisi—the lovely Umbrian hill town that had been home to St. Francis, famous for his love of birds and other wildlife—for the Easter weekend; at dawn on Sunday, we were awakened by a great blasting of shotguns, for just beyond our window, which overlooked the town wall and the woods beyond, the hunting hordes were mercilessly shooting at everything that peeped or fluttered. During the weeks of the migration of birds from Africa to Italy, the meat counter of the *supermercato* we patronized in Florence displayed row upon row of bits of fluff, from each of which extended a limp neck and a little head with frozen beak and lidded eyes. Shooting as they came, hunters marched through the villa groves and fields; soon the pervasive migrant melody was stilled, leaving only the song of the pair of nightingales that lived in the bushes by the little family chapel. Though hunters sought out nightingales as a special delicacy, our landlady said that they were apt to survive longer than other birds because at least some of them had the good sense to nest in thick shrubbery close to houses—but here, of course, the cats eventually got them.

Occasionally we had dinner at Omero's, a restaurant on our side of the Arno; it was on the crest of a hill not far from the Torre del Gallo, where Galileo built his telescope and made his astronomical observations. To provide guests with a fine vista of Florence and the Arno valley, the proprietor had put the dining room in the rear of the building; diners entered the restaurant through a storeroom door, making a passage beneath the cured hams and other meats hanging from ceiling hooks. Remote from the conventional tourist routes, Omero's served good food at reasonable prices and attracted (we were told) young actors, artists, and clothing designers—something that seemed to us probably true, since a majority of the diners were in their twenties or thirties, many of them fashionably dressed, and nearly all of them wore dark glasses even at night.

One evening at Omero's, we had a misunderstanding with our waiter that, while based on language, surely was connected with a difference in cultural assumptions about animals. Nobody in our family could finish the unusually generous servings; enough remained on our plates to provide us with a meal at home the following day. Did we have the temerity to ask our waiter to put it in a container? In America one asks for a doggie bag, and I thought such a euphemism might be customary in much of the world—and certainly would be understood at a restaurant like Omero's.

As our waiter, who spoke some English, cleared the table for dessert, I asked him if we could have a doggie bag. "*Che cosa?*" he asked, puzzled. I was the only member of my family not studying Italian at one school or another. Cris, who was enrolled in several classes at the British Institute, was further along in the language than was Jean, who took a class in Italian for foreigners at the University of Florence, or Jimmy, a student at a day school for American children.

"*Un saco,*" Cris said, pointing to the food on each of our plates. The waiter remained bewildered. "*Non capisco,*" he said.

"*Per il cane,*" Cris said.

"*Un saco per il cane?*" The phrase obviously made no sense to him.

While the waiter watched intently, Cris went through a pantomime: he opened an invisible bag and, lifting first one plate and then another, pretended to push food into it with a knife.

"*Capisco,*" the waiter cried, striking his brow with his hand as illumination came.

At first, it wasn't clear to us what that insight consisted of, since he didn't give us a doggie bag with the check. Perhaps, in Italy, domestic animals are unlikely to be treated as members of the family, and who could think that a bag for the dog could really be intended for people? The waiter must have assumed that we had gone into animal husbandry in a big American way on a Tuscan estate; for, as we were preparing to enter our car, he staggered out of the restaurant after us with two huge plastic bags filled with the day's kitchen scrapings. He smiled so radiantly for being of such assistance to us in providing food for our pigs or other farm animals if not for a kennel filled with ravenous hunting dogs that I couldn't tell him we didn't want all that garbage, and not even Cris had the facility with the language to explain that Maria, the gatekeeper's wife, would be furious with us for making her build a fire huge enough to incinerate all of those scrapings in order to prevent the officials from arresting our landlady for renting out her villa to a horde of tourists without paying the proper tax.

As it was, I opened the trunk, and would have helped him lift the bags into it had he not waved me off; I even offered him an additional tip, which he—possessor of an Italian generosity of soul—refused. Hoping to find a rubbish bin into which we might furtively dispose of our garbage, I drove slowly back to our villa; but Italians are too canny to leave any such receptacles near the curb. For several days, dark smoke rose from the hidden area where Maria burned our garbage; though she was normally a friendly woman, she muttered and shook her head when I encountered her by our door, and it was a week or two before she again smiled and waved at us as we passed the gate house.

In general, Italians are a warm-hearted people, the men as well as the women showing an understanding of, and affection for, anybody's babies and young children that far exceeds my own. But I met only two Italians who treated their domestic animals as comrades; these Italians seemed like Americans, and their example made me yearn for home. During that year-long residency in Florence, I became conscious for the first time in my life that the value I found in animals was part of the particular culture I had been born into.

II. MY BIRD

The eleventh edition of *The Encyclopedia Britannica,* one that humanists value over subsequent editions for its subjective judgments on all sorts of quirky topics, says of the mockingbird (a native American species) that while there is little about the bird's physical appearance "beyond its graceful form to recommend it," its melody possesses "a varied range and liquid fullness of tone that are unequalled, according to its admirers, even by those of the nightingale."

Several years after our return from Florence, a pair of mockingbirds made a journey farther north and west than is customary for the species to nest in foliage near our house. In the mornings, the male would perch on the chimney serving the Franklin stove in my study, his melody coming down the flue to resonate in the metal belly of that stove. Later in the *Encyclopedia Britannica* article, the author proves himself to be one of the bird's admirers by saying outright that its melody far surpasses that of "its European rival," a judgment that struck me as wholly true, as I compared the song of *my* mockingbird with that of the nightingale cock in Italy, whose melancholic gurglings had seemed to me an acknowledgment of impending demise. While plagiarizing at will from the work of others in the manner of all self-confident artists, my bird, through improvisation and surprising combinations, ended up with compositions totally his own. By making not the nightingale's but the mockingbird's melody a metaphor for the creative faculty, I put myself one up on Keats. I came to expect that morning serenade, which gave me the emotional kick—and more than that, the hubris—I needed for the day's work.

But one morning the melody stopped. On the front porch, I discovered my favorite cat, Lucifer, sitting next to the gift offering she had left me—the severed head of my favorite bird. She ceased being my favorite cat at that instant. I chased that cat around the house maybe three times, vainly burrowing after her into the bushes. For the remainder of that long summer, the surviving mate spent her hours on the backyard power line, singing over and over a dirge—several notes, monotonously repeated, that drifted into my study through the open window. "Damn you, listen to that," I cried to Lucifer, whenever she stood at the study door in a cautious test of the emotional waters within.

My work at the desk most of the summer was not very productive. It occurred to me, one sultry afternoon, that the casual or indifferent attitude of Italians toward animals is in some ways preferable to my own attempt at a more intimate kinship. Such an insight didn't grant me an Italian insouciance toward cats, but it did permit me to welcome Lucifer back into the good graces of the family and to get on with the task at hand.

III. ANTHROPOMORPHISM

Some months back, my local newspaper, *The Ithaca Journal,* carried a feature story about a Cornell veterinarian who specializes in animal behavior. According to that article, she often finds the key to a pet's behavior problem in its owner. While animals share with humans such emotions as "fear, courage, trust, love, hatred, aggression," humans and their pets may have different responses to any given situation. She is quoted as saying that veterinarians in the animal behavior clinic at Cornell "try to look at the way an animal interacts with its owner," and frequently discover that owners "are anthropomorphic, meaning they try to give their animals the same values they have."

The observation seems unexceptional: you need to find out the reason that a cat pisses on the rug instead of getting angry at it for doing something you don't, even as you shouldn't expect a cat to know that the bird it killed was a metaphor to you. As an owner of pets for more than sixty years, though, I think the comment implies too sweeping an indictment of anthropomorphism. Perhaps because of an early incident that led to a bonding between animal and owner, some pets seem to *want* to be considered human. Animals and humans have the same biological drives; animals are simply more transparent in demonstrating them. (Scoldings, threats, strong ropes, and even locked doors failed to keep Ben, an Irish setter my family once owned, from consummation of his sexual desires; on one occasion, he dug out a large foundation stone to reach a neighbor's bitch locked in the basement, on another he leaped with virile abandon through an expensive stained glass window of a house a mile from his own. When an official of the SPCA recommended castration, I felt a pain in my own testicles.)

Furthermore, I believe that an animal and a human sometimes do share identical attitudes toward an experience; that the animal can communicate such attitudes to a person through intimate eye contact as well as through body language; and that, once expressed, those attitudes can form the basis of a lifetime of understanding between the pair. As best as I can describe in words a communication that is wholly visual, the intelligence that passes from animal to human is based on humor and tolerance; it is as if the animal understands that he and his human companion are engaged in a friendly conspiracy.

Until Tammy, his beloved stablemate, died of old age, Smoky (walleyed though horses are) frequently communicated that sort of message to me. As a mischievous young horse, Smoky acted as if he intended to bite my arm whenever I slipped a rubber pail of grain under the bottom rail of his stall; to outwit him, I would pretend to put it in the stall, and as he came for the grain (or my flesh) I would quickly place the bucket in the space outside the stall. My strategy became part of a game we played together: he would warily wait between the two possible positions, while I made a feint with the bucket toward one or the other. But would he really bite me if I left my arm exposed as he rushed toward the bucket, baring his great teeth? One morning, after engaging in the customary feints, I left my arm in a vulnerable position, just above the bucket. He bared his teeth—and, after delicately nipping my skin, nuzzled my arm and then licked it with his leathery tongue. Before bending his head into the grain bucket, he gave me for the first time that friendly and conspiratorial look.

Tammy died in the neighboring stall one day. She weighed half a ton; it took a couple of pulleys attached to barn beams and a winch-equipped truck to remove the body. Jean and I managed to entice the nervous Smoky into the pasture, shutting the gate connecting it with the paddock and barn and covering the fence with blankets, in a vain attempt to keep him from seeing the body being slowly dragged toward the truck. Despite such tactics, Smoky held me accountable for the loss. Before the death, he would whinny when I approached the paddock with a carrot or apple. After Tammy's body was trucked away, he not only didn't whinny, he refused to take the food. He even turned his head away: he simply would not look at me. A year passed before he would accept anything from my hand. But our games belong wholly to the past, and his eyes now tell me nothing at all.

Were Smoky and I to have a consultation with the animal behaviorist at the Cornell clinic because of my complaint that my old horse no longer communicates with me, she might consider me an egregious example of anthropomorphism. Is it possible that all along I only imagined an intelligent, if purely visual, understanding between Smoky and me that had formed the basis of a relationship? Had I only imagined that now and then I had seen the same look of conspiratorial friendship in nearly all the animals I've known since childhood? Like a trust in God or in the unity underlying everything in the phenomenal universe, one's belief in such a matter resists conclusive proof. I can only say that whenever I see that look, my memory carries me back to an incident in my childhood that—at least for me—validates its truth.

In this memory, I am eleven years old, lying on my stomach outside the side door of a marvelous house in a new addition— called Normandy by its developers—of Little Rock; recently, my father, a traveling salesman, has deserted my mother, my brother, and me for a widow in San Antonio. It is a sunny day of a long summer during one of the years of the Great Depression, and my father has sent us too little money. Soon the three of us and my dog—a black German shepherd named Bruin by my mother, since as a puppy he resembled a bear cub—will have to leave that house, which is being repossessed, to drive a thousand miles north, where we will arrive, without advance warning, at the home of some relatives. Bruin was my father's last gift to me before his betrayal of his family.

The ground is pleasantly warm on my belly on this day. Bruin is standing above me, ready for a little game we play that always makes my mother angry at both of us, for it often ends up with a rip in my pants that she will have to mend. It's not much of a game, really: I give a little ass-wiggle, and Bruin—already an unusually large and strong dog, even for a German shepherd— attempts to lift me up by the seat of my pants. On this occasion, I give the customary sign and he obediently tugs at my pants. Suddenly, though, he lets me drop and assumes an innocent sitting posture at my side. I look up to see my mother's face above us, at the kitchen window. Apparently sharp-eyed Bruin has seen her before she has noticed what we have been up to; instead of scolding us, she smiles and waves. I sit up, facing Bruin; his eyes are friendly and intelligent, full of the knowledge of our conspiracy. To share such a secret with a loyal companion gives me great happiness: it is happiness of the sort I imagine I would feel if, waking in the middle of the night, I heard my father's car once more turning into the driveway.

Whatever anthropomorphism I can be accused of has its source in this moment.

IV. GOATS AS A TEST OF HUMAN CHARACTER

Larry, who is forty, and my namesake Jim, who is thirty, both live in New York City, where both are employed in film; Cris, the middle son, now works at Cornell, as do Jean and I, and shares the large farmhouse with us. Cris returned home a number of years ago because we had fields available for the six goats he had just purchased—the nucleus of a herd he needed for the goat milk and cheese he hoped to produce. At the time he was working the night shift at Morse Chain in Ithaca, and dreaming of a more pastoral vocation. The goat barn that he built, one with a milking parlor and a large processing room as well as eating and sleeping quarters for the forty-odd goats he ultimately owned, now stands vacant, at the far end of the grassy field that constitutes our backyard; for the financial returns from that enterprise were never enough to allow him to quit his factory job, and the dairy work was too time-consuming to permit him to continue with it while holding down a full-time job.

Goats may not have memories as long-lasting and detailed as those of horses, who remember not only deaths but something as mundane as a random route they once were directed to take through a woods; nevertheless, goats are more canny in their utilization of past experiences. As a two-year-old, Smoky felt the sting of the electric fence surrounding his pasture and consequently he has never attempted to get beyond that barrier, though the charger has been disconnected for maybe a decade; on the other hand, Cris's goats soon figured out that the electricity pulsed through the wires, and scrambled at will through the fence in the interval between pulses. Within a week of the arrival of the first goats, we lost to them a small orchard of young apple trees which just were beginning to bear their first fruit; within the month we lost the long row of lilac bushes bordering the farm road leading to our barns and the old apple orchard—now mainly taken over by walnuts—beyond. Today, two blue spruces in the backyard still carry the hourglass shape sculpted into them by goats standing on their hind legs to browse upon the succulent branches.

But goats—especially the kids—are endearing creatures, and their damage never vexed Jean or me very long. Not even Cris, whatever his labor and ultimate disappointment, regretted the four years that goats shared our lives as well as our efforts at landscaping. One winter eleven kids were born, and the barn, despite heat lamps, was so cold that early each morning Cris, whose shift ended at midnight, brought two or three into the house, sometimes after assisting the mother in a particularly difficult birth. We kept them in the kitchen, the only room with a linoleum floor. At 7 A.M., while Cris slept, Jean and I fed them with nursing bottles and then watched them frolic about the room for half an hour or so before we put them back into a makeshift pen in the corner of the room and mopped up the floor.

Cris developed an affection toward his herd, including a love for its littler creatures; but anybody who raises goats—or cows, for that matter—as part of a dairy operation would be incapable of continuing were he or she to impart to them human attributes. By and large, male kids are economically useless and must be slaughtered; insufficiently productive females must be culled from the herd. Because the milk is intended for sale or for the production of cheeses, kids must be immediately taken from their mothers and weaned to a bottle: once they get nourishment from the udder, it is difficult to convince them to suckle from a nursing bottle containing a milk replacement. Even the first fluid from the udder—the protection-giving colostrum—must be given by bottle.

Cris learned much about goat husbandry from three veteran goat raisers. He bought his initial goats from a locally famous psychic or witch whose hands had become too arthritic for her to continue milking, and soon he became a friend of a long-married couple from Colombia who had bought a small farm overlooking Ithaca for the purpose of operating a large-scale goat dairy—eventually they had a herd of over two hundred animals. On the basis of my own limited experience with these three people, I decided that goat raisers are unusual people. The psychic had a confidence in her occult powers to abet her handling of animals as well as humans. ("Did you do that?" her husband asked her in anger, on the night that the television set, a source of controversy between them, blew up. She told me about this incident—leaving her husband's question unanswered—on a hot Sunday afternoon as she was using the forked branch of a sapling to find us a new water supply, since our well had proved inadequate to the thirst of Cris's growing herd: a well drilled at the spot she indicated hit an underground, if slightly sulfurous, Mississippi.) Though they were in their seventies, the Colombian couple still practiced yoga, and often were standing on their heads on those early mornings that Cris arrived with a problem about goats.

Successful goat raisers obviously were able to combine attachment with non-attachment, subjectivity with objectivity, affection with a businesslike attitude—a mental approach that seemed to combine Italian attitudes toward animals with my own, and that, whatever its metaphysical catalyst, was the only practical way to handle creatures that are cunning in both senses of the word. Cris had the required intuitive knack. Still, he continually told me, as if in reminder to himself, that to avoid a hassle and heartbreak with animals, you simply couldn't consider them to be like people—advice similar to that later offered by the animal behaviorist at Cornell.

Only once, to my knowledge, did he violate that injunction, and it came near the end of his dairy enterprise, in a moment of exhaustion. How does one whose hours are limited find the time and the energy to milk goats and market that milk, to experiment with methods of making various exotic cheeses, to treat the ailments of the herd, to serve as midwife during difficult births? In his attempt to cope, Cris for a time brought a partner into the business, a young woman who took over the milking as well as the decisions concerning which goats to keep, and in addition hired a part-time helper, an exceptionally gentle young man. On a Saturday night in early spring, several kids were born, with Cris and his helper in attendance. At midnight, as Jean and I were preparing for bed, Cris ran into the house in great distress, shouting, "I just injured a kid!"

Cornell has clinics for both large and small animals; "large," though, includes all livestock, and so its veterinarians treat sheep and goats as well as horses and cows and an occasional lion or elephant. Cris called the large animal clinic's emergency number. None of the veterinarians who had treated his goats in the past was on duty that night, but Cris was known and liked by them. The call was transferred to the home of one of the goat specialists, and he agreed to be waiting at the clinic when Cris arrived with the newborn kid.

After he made the call, Cris told us what had happened. He and his helper were trying to get the kids to nurse from bottles. While his back was turned, his helper—whose kid was resisting the plastic nipple—decided it was in their mutual welfare to let it nurse in the way intended by nature. Cris took the kid from the mother, and for half an hour tried unsuccessfully to coax it to take the colostrum from the bottle. Finally, in frustration with his helper, the kid, and perhaps the whole bloody business, he roughly shoved the kid from his lap. It hit the wall, and couldn't walk. Perhaps its hindquarters were paralyzed, perhaps there was a spinal injury.

Most of us have felt such impulses; with our own children, we resist them as best we can. In his remorse, Cris had exaggerated both his violence and the injury; the kid was not seriously hurt. Actually, the event provided me with one of the most emotionally rewarding moments in my experience. I accompanied Cris in his pickup truck to the clinic, holding on my lap the cardboard box which contained the kid and the soft rags cushioning it against bumps. A mixture of rain and soft snow was falling, making it hard to see. The doors of the clinic were immense enough to permit the entry of the largest truck. Inside, it seemed a gigantic and immaculate barn, brightly illuminated. For some reason, a veterinarian, his white coat stained with blood or manure, was marching a cow back and forth. A blue-jeaned young woman was sleeping on some hay outside a stall; apparently the crisis with her horse was over, for the animal was peacefully munching. From another stall, a bull gazed at us. He was as immobile as the bronze memorial statue of a horse enclosed by a fence I once had seen in a Kentucky pasture.

Cris's veterinarian, a slender man in his middle years who had donned a freshly laundered white coat, watched us approach down the major aisle, which, lined by the stalls and with the roof trusses above, reminded me of a cathedral nave. Cris put the little box at his feet. The veterinarian bent over the kid, lifting it from the box to observe its attempt to walk. He gently probed the animal's hindquarters with his fingers. Only one rear leg now seemed to drag, and the kid was able to put weight even on that one.

"What happened?" the veterinarian asked.

Cris said, "She wouldn't suckle from the bottle. I got angry, and threw her against the wall."

If I had been in my son's position, I would have prefaced

that confession with all the extenuating circumstances I could think of. It's possible I might even have lied, saying, maybe, a horse stepped on it, or I just don't know what happened. The veterinarian looked at Cris, his eyes (I thought) unusually kind.

"That kind of thing happens more often than you probably realize," he said. "Your kid is luckier than most; it was just a minor dislocation, and the joint's back in place."

I was astonished. "You fixed it, that fast?"

"As you can see, it wasn't much of a problem," the veterinarian said. "By tomorrow the limp should be gone."

A smiling, gray-haired woman encountered us just outside the clinic door. Despite the hour, she had come to see the progress of some animal of hers—a cow or a sheep. Cris had dispensed with the box, and was holding the kid in his arms. The outside floodlight illuminated all of us, and the falling snow as well. "What a cute kid!" the woman exclaimed, fondling its ears. And to me she said, "Your jacket is so handsome!" It was made of a beige-colored plastic and had a rip under one arm; I had bought it long ago at Woolworth. But the wet plastic did look attractive in the glow of the floodlight, and I've remembered the praise of that jacket as a kind of benediction—as if I were an aging father and maybe grandparent who had been blessed in an unusual way.

V. SPIRITUAL LOVE

In my childhood, the stars and planets burned much more brightly in the night sky than they do now. Atmospheric pollution accounts for much, but not all, of the difference, for some of it is subjective. When I was eight or nine, my parents bought for me and my older brother, Jack, a children's encyclopedia, *Our*

Wonder World, that contained many conundrums, examples of word play, and the like; among the many illustrations were the first large photographs I had seen of star clusters and of planets in our solar system. In Little Rock during that first summer of my father's departure, I was fascinated by those photographs and by the text that accompanied them; as evening came on, Bruin and I would lie together on the lawn of that house in Normandy we were destined to leave, and I would tell him about the Martian canals, the moons of Jupiter, the rings around Saturn, the speed of light, and the nature of the universe. Whether he ever saw the Milky Way, I don't know; but on occasions he obediently looked skyward, and I could see unknown stars reflected in his dark eyes.

I've heard it said of passionate love that it is narcissistic; that is to say, the lover does not see the beloved as she or he truly is, but as a mirror of the lover's own spiritual desires, as a manifestation of idealistic yearnings. To discover an analogy between the love potion that drew Tristan to Iseult in doomed passion and the moment of shared understanding that linked me to Bruin may be an absurd reduction of a major myth of Western civilization, but my delusion was at least of the same kind as Tristan's: grand animal though he was, Bruin for me became more than an animal or human can ever be. My anthropomorphic error was not one of imputing my own responses to him, but of making him a representation of an ideal beyond my grasp—something perhaps rationally less difficult to do with an animal than with a person, which may account for the deification of animals in early cultures, not only in Egypt but throughout a human world still in close contact with a natural one.

Our attitudes toward animals change with our own altering views toward much else, and mine have changed with the inevitable ebbing of the once insatiable wanting that sometimes makes an unholy—and perhaps uniquely American—trinity of soul, sex, and possessions. For decades, though, Bruin reigned as such a major myth figure in my personal animal kingdom that I wanted any new animal to be as much like him as possible. The dog that we currently own, a black Labrador retriever-German shepherd mix named Gandolf, was a gift from Cris's former goat partner, who was leaving Ithaca for California. When the dog was offered to us by telephone, I said I probably didn't want it, but upon seeing Gandy, I immediately decided that we should take her—simply because her ears, when she raised them in alert attention, were black sails identical to those of Bruin, dead for fifty years.

After my mother, brother, and I had to leave Normandy, I feared I might be forced to give up Bruin. My mother's sister and her husband took us into their home in Lakewood, Ohio, and allowed the dog to sleep in the basement. I punished his every indiscretion, not only out of fear that his misbehavior might cause his exile, but also because such misbehavior was not in keeping with the expectations of my love. Once, by a confectionery store at the corner of Madison and McKinley Avenues, Bruin picked a fight with a much smaller dog, and I hit him so severely that a woman stopped her car to shout at me, "If you strike that magnificent animal one more time, I'll call the police!" Her accusation of brutality shocked me, for it was nothing but love that had made me treat him like that. She didn't know that in Little Rock I had protected Bruin from exhaustion by keeping him in the house whenever I knew my brother intended to practice with golf clubs or rifle, for Bruin was ever eager to retrieve objects, and his hearing and eyesight were so acute that he could return with every golf ball, and once (my brother said) even found the tree in which a bullet was embedded. Nor did that woman know that Bruin would never repeat a transgression I had punished him for. In Arkansas, while we were companions on a long walk, Bruin had outraged me by killing a chicken. He saw a flock of chickens in an unfenced yard, sent them into a frenzy by rushing at them before I could tell him to stop, and shook one dead in his mouth. He dropped the corpse during my homeward pursuit of him. I hit and scolded him before locking him in the garage, and withheld his supper. Subsequently, whenever we passed the yard with the chickens, he crossed to the other side of the street, to be as far from temptation as he could get.

In my fifteenth year, my mother and I accompanied my brother to Flint, Michigan, for he had been admitted to General Motors Institute, where students could earn an engineering degree while getting practical experience as well as a salary by working in one of the numerous General Motors plants then located in Flint. The only apartment we could afford was on the second floor of a downtown house whose landlady forbade pets. My father's sister and her husband, who lived in Westerville, Ohio, agreed to take Bruin. My brother made a sturdy wooden box in accordance with Railway Express instructions; but it was I who betrayed Bruin by coaxing him into it. He gave me a pleading look, but obeyed me. "Now, go get the form from your mother so we can leave," one of the two Railway Express employees said to me. "What form?" the other one asked; I knew from the question that it was a kindly ruse to keep me from seeing a boxed and frightened Bruin being lifted into the truck. I stood at the hall window by the staircase leading to our apartment long after the truck disappeared.

When my uncle and aunt picked up Bruin at the Railway Express office—they had to come for him, for the company refused to deliver him by truck—they found a snarling and dehydrated animal whose box was plastered with cautionary signs: apparently he had bitten a handler en route, and afterwards was not given either food or water. As I knew from their letters, my relatives grew to respect Bruin's intelligence and bravery. The most remarkable instance of these was his rescue of the neighbor's dog, a small female, that had fallen into a creek swollen by the spring rains. My uncle wrote that Bruin saved her by jumping into the torrent, grabbing her by the neck fur, and swimming with her to safety. That sounded like a fictional exploit in a Lassie novel: could it really be true? Yes, since Bruin, my admirable dog, was the savior. But Bruin, through this exploit and others, became my uncle's admirable dog.

I was to see him again only once, and not until he was old and I a college junior. My uncle and aunt had moved to a suburb of Akron, and I was visiting them in their new home. My uncle was away on a trip the day I came, and Bruin and my aunt met me at the door of a tidy two-story house. Bruin's ears were up, the two black sails separated by puzzled furrows of fur. He didn't wag his tail as I stroked him. Suddenly, though, he embarrassed me by sniffing vigorously at my buttocks. Excretory odors are agents of memory in dogs, no doubt for Odysseus' Argus as well as my childhood companion, though it is a detail that Homer ignores. At the instant of recognition, Bruin—how it delighted me!—leaped at me to lick my face; unable to contain his happiness, he jumped on the coffee table, upsetting all the glass objects on it. He ran through the dining room and kitchen, circling back to leap at me again, and then up the stairs, where he jumped on or over the beds, tables, and chairs in every room. My aunt and I followed him upstairs as quickly as we could—to prevent further damage, I suppose, but also just to see the antic behavior. We laughed until we embraced each other, crying.

Six months later, Bruin died. In his letter telling me of the death, my uncle said he had a worrisome feeling that a nutritional lack might have caused it; he and my aunt hadn't been able to afford more than a can of dog food each day, to supplement table scraps. I suppose he as well as I never really thought about the fact that Bruin would die: you come to expect immortality from a dog like that, and feel a personal responsibility when the animal proves as mortal as you. It was in keeping with the narcissism of my old love for him that I wondered if he had died because, having been so joyously reunited with me, he felt once again betrayed, this time by my return to college. But Bruin was eleven, my age when my father gave him to me; and at eleven a large dog has lived his normal span.

In recent years, conscious of a diminution of my spiritual powers, I have remembered again and again a passage in an essay on old age by Francis Bacon: "A certain rabbin, upon the text, 'Your young men shall see visions, and your old men shall dream dreams,' inferreth that young men are admitted nearer to God than old." At sixty-nine, I know that the soul is a name for our unobtainable desires, and that as a child I made of Bruin a repository of a vast wanting that included my absent father but went beyond that to reach the stars—a mighty wish to reach a spiritual truth beyond my limited self, one that could end my isolation by merging me with the natural world and the mysteries of the universe.

Over the decades, I dispersed the qualities I associated with

Bruin to every animal that came into my household until little was left to give away, other than the alert nobility of his black ears. To recall the strength of a childhood wanting makes me nostalgic for it, but its loss probably has made me gentler with my animals.

VI. WRATH

When Gandy entered our household, she immediately became friendly with another black animal, a female cat missing a front leg whose name, ironically enough, was Grabber. She had been given that name by Cris's goat dairy partner, who had gone to the SPCA shelter with Cris in search of a barn cat. The kitten had actually chosen them, by reaching through the bars of the cage to grab the partner's sleeve as she and Cris passed by. Following the collapse of the dairy enterprise, Grabber became a house cat that I fed. For three days, including one that was the coldest of the winter, she was absent from home. She came back at last, one of her front legs hurt so badly that it became gangrenous. The veterinarian who finally amputated it—for several days Cris massaged the leg in warm water in a vain attempt to return the blood circulation—said the injury had been inflicted by an animal trap.

Given Grabber's new vulnerability, her ready trust of a strange animal—so much larger than she, and a member of a frequently hostile species—surprised and gratified Jean and Cris and me. Gandy, though, is an unusually gentle creature, and at first probably felt an insecurity within an environment still alien to her, so perhaps from the beginning a mutual need led them to sleep together on the carpet of the downstairs bathroom. Waking at 2 or 3 A.M., Jean and I could see in the glow of the bathroom nightlight the cat curled up against the warm belly of the dog. Gandy didn't seem to sleep as soundly as Grabber; if we stirred in bed, she would thump her tail, without moving the rest of her body. It was as if she remained as alert as possible, in protection of her smaller, three-legged friend—though in thinking that I probably am giving the dog some feelings of my own.

I have always detested the use of steel traps to capture animals, and it angered me not only that somebody had set one or more of them, without permission, somewhere on our farmlands, which extend a half mile in nearly every direction from our house, but would permit an animal caught in a trap to suffer there for as many days as our cat obviously had. In the days and weeks after the amputation, Cris and I searched fruitlessly for traps on the property. Just before dawn one spring morning, I stepped over the sleeping pair to get to the toilet. As I was returning to bed, I remembered a newspaper report that a comet would be visible before sunrise that day, and so I put on a bathrobe, got the binoculars from the bookcase beneath the window that faces the bird feeder, and went to the glassed-in porch to have a look. But instead of focusing on the tiny golden smudge in the eastern sky, I used the binoculars to magnify a rusty pickup truck parked a quarter mile down the road, near the hedgerow that marks a stream meandering through our fields, just as its owner emerged from the hedgerow, a limp muskrat in each hand.

Without taking time to throw on any clothing under my bathrobe, I grabbed my car keys, ran to the car, and sent the gravel flying as I backed out of the driveway. The trapper, having figured out I was the owner of the property he was poaching upon, and maybe sensing from my speed a murderous intent, jumped into his pickup and took off. Ignoring the stop sign, he spun his truck left at the dangerous intersection with the state highway, and I did the same with my little Horizon. Apparently his instinct was to make it home, as if he would find safety there; he braked so suddenly for his driveway I almost crashed into his rear bumper. He was out of his truck and running for his door as I jumped from my car, shouting, "Stop! Stop right where you are!" a command that he instantly obeyed.

Rage made me incoherent, and nearly blind. I told him he had caught God knows how many of my dogs in his vicious traps (an exaggerated and maybe wholly untrue indictment: two of our dogs in recent years had limped home with leg wounds less severe than Grabber's) and had caused my cat to lose her leg, and what ever had given him the cruelty to trespass on my land? Gradually, I saw him for what he was: a frail man considerably older than I who was trembling from palsy or fright, the owner of a truck missing a fender and with a hood held down by a rope; who lived in an unpainted house—that place of his refuge—so unprepossessing that I had never given it the slightest notice in passing by it nearly every day for many years. Head down, he begged my pardon. His wife was dead, his children gone. For most of his life, he had been self-employed, a handyman, and now his income came from muskrat furs and welfare checks. He always intended to inspect his traps every dawn, but these past months had frequently been bedridden, and hadn't he gotten up this morning to check them, feverish though he was? He didn't know anything about the dogs, but he was terribly sorry about the cat.

I used to think now and again about the contrary aspects—the gentleness and the grimness—of the religion I had been born into but had rejected. It seemed to me that if a merciful and omnipotent God existed, Hell could not: for if God knew everything about causality—if He had the answer to every "Why?"—He surely would have to forgive even the most terrible of human crimes. In the present case, I was not God but an animal lover holding the flaps of a robe together.

I said, "Get some Havahart traps—you know, the kind that just cage the muskrats—and you can leave them anywhere you want on my land."

He said he couldn't afford them. If that was the case, I said, he'd better not return with his traps to my property, for I would confiscate them; stern as I tried to sound, I felt sorrier for him than I did for the cat he had victimized, who at this moment probably was still sleeping against the belly of a friend.

But relationships between animals, like those between people, can quickly sour. Grabber disappeared a few weeks later, never to return, two days after the night Gandy nearly killed her. Jean and I were awakened by a cry that reminded me of the rabbit's scream as the peasant in Italy drove the pointed stick through its eye to its brain. Grabber was doing the screaming, for she was dangling from Gandy's jaws. At my shout, the dog dropped the cat and assumed an abject posture while the cat scrambled on her three legs to the safety of the basement. "One or the other of them must have had a frightening dream that started the attack," Jean said; but my first thought was, We have but ourselves, and even I find a terrible pleasure in the chase: who or what can save us now? In hindsight, I suppose such a cryptic thought came to me because for a frightening instant I had lost those assumptions of personal integrity and conscience that had enabled me to accept the absence of God from our tangled human affairs. Such a loss can occur when we see ourselves merely as beasts, while denying any quality but brutishness to our fellow animals.

VII. THE ROAD TO THE VETERINARY HOSPITAL

On a balmy night in late June last summer, I sat next to Gandy on the huge slab of slate that, with a thinner slab for a step, probably has served as a front door stoop since 1831, the year our house was built. Humans and some of the unregenerate (or at least undomesticated) animals live at cross purposes, and generations of burrowing rodents—rats, mice, squirrels, chipmunks—have undermined some of the rocks that support that slab, causing it to break under its own weight. One of the sections had begun to tilt. From what distance had Thomas Kelsey, who built this house from the white pines cleared for his farmlands, carted this stone, and how had he managed to get it in place? And how could I bring the broken pieces (each of them probably weighed nearly as much as had Tammy, whose body had been so difficult to move from the stable) into alignment before winter ice caused Jean or me to fall? The latter concern is one that wouldn't have come into my mind when I was younger, and only did now because Jean had broken a knee in another kind of accident a few years earlier.

Our house is at a country crossroads, and neither road—one dirt, one blacktop—carries much traffic at night. I listened to the frogs in our pond, diagonally across the intersection from the house but hidden by the highbush cranberries Jean and I had received as plantings from a state conservation agency as a source of food for the birds—though to my knowledge no bird (and no person other than that renowned advocate of wild food, the late

Euell Gibbons) ever relished the bitter fruit. Over the years, the pond—where we and our children used to swim—has silted up; maybe future owners of our property would reclaim it for their children.

Why think about such problems on this pleasant and sweet-smelling night? I watched the random pattern of the fireflies, the headlights of a tractor in the field across the road (the neighboring farmer who rents much of our land was working late, baling and collecting hay before the promised rain arrived), and the regular sweep of the searchlight across the clouds, a beacon calling attention to the annual Enfield Firemen's Fair in a field by a busier crossroads—Miller's Corners—three miles away. When our children were young, Jean and I used to take them to that fair, to ride the Ferris wheel and merry-go-round or to try their skill at a variety of games. Once Cris, watching people fruitlessly trying to win goldfish by throwing table tennis balls at the tiny bowls containing them, figured out how to gain so many fish that Jean and I had to buy him an aquarium, for even at ten he had a scientific bent of mind. Instead of throwing the balls, he tossed them, underhanded, high in the air, so that they plopped into the bowls instead of glancing off the rims; after he'd won a half dozen or so, the proprietor of the stand shooed him away and shut down his business long enough for those waiting in line who had observed his technique to wander off to the shooting gallery or to the pie raffle.

Like those of many classical revival farmhouses in upstate New York, the woodshed of our house is actually built into one of the wings; it has a sliding barn-type exterior door, and another that opens into the kitchen. In the summers, our dogs have always slept in the woodshed with the exterior door open; their presence there keeps rabbits and raccoons out of the nearby vegetable garden. I was walking with Gandy toward the wood-shed just as the farmer drove out of the field, his task completed. The tractor headlights lit the bare branches of the line of Russian olives I planted by the roadside a quarter century before to give privacy to the backyard with its picnic table. Those little trees with their shimmering leaves fortunately had never proved appetizing to the goats, and so had given seclusion to our summer suppers outdoors for maybe twenty years; but now most of them were dead. When they first showed signs of dying, I talked to an old acquaintance, a now retired nurseryman in the nearby hamlet of Mecklenburg, thinking he might know of some antidote for the road salt that I believed was harming them; it shocked me to learn from him that Russian olives (unlike autumn olives, some of which we also had planted, or highbush cranberries) normally live less than twenty-five years. But those trees would at least provide us with some firewood, whenever I got around to cutting them up with a chain saw. It is always a help to think of a new use for something that has died or outlived its purpose: it pleased Jean and me to use the backstop of Jimmy's old baseball diamond as a support for our pole beans.

The tractor puttered down the road, pulling two wagons loaded with the hay that had been ejected into them by the farmer's new hay baler. For years, he had been opposed to such a labor-saving device, simply because he liked the bales of hay to be placed neatly in the wagons, the way a farmer and his sturdy sons can stack them; his new baler piled them randomly, an affront to his sense of order. But his sons, like mine, were grown, his with farms of their own. As I left Gandy in the woodshed, lightning flared up in the northern sky, but thunder never followed, and the rains never came.

The smallest details of that night remain in my mind, the

events transferred from my short-term memory to the one that will last as long as I do; for in the early hours of the morning Gandy, like Grabber before her, lost a front leg—and part of the shoulder as well. She happened to be on the dirt road—was she in pursuit of a rabbit who had entered our garden?—just as a car came down it, perhaps the only car on that road from midnight to dawn. Jean and I were awakened by a cry of dog-anguish; we ran to the front door just as Gandy reached it. She collapsed in the hallway. The motorist who had hit her stopped his car in front of the house long enough to see we had admitted the dog, and then drove off.

The commotion woke Cris. While Jean and I tried to stem the flow of blood with towels, Cris dialed the emergency number of the Cornell small animal clinic, and explained the nature of the injury to one of the veterinary students on duty that morning. She said she would contact a surgeon, and instructed us to tie a rope around Gandy's muzzle: severely injured dogs, however gentle they normally are, sometimes bite as they are being lifted. Cris made an emergency litter from a canvas cot. We put no rope on Gandy's muzzle. Gently we put her on that litter and carried her to the bed of Cris's pickup truck. Jean and I climbed into the bed with her; Jean wrapped blankets around Gandy's body, to prevent her from being chilled by the wind as we traveled.

Gandy was making strange noises, and twisting her body on the litter; Jean kneeled on one side of her and I on the other, to keep her secure. I stroked her head, and the ears that were like Bruin's. And so we headed for Ithaca, and the veterinary hospital on the far side of town. We passed the hedgerow where I'd seen the trapper while looking for a comet. Cris turned left on the state highway as I had done in my pursuit of the poacher; half a mile down the highway, we passed the house where I had managed to catch him. Other people now lived in it: I supposed the trapper was dead. At Miller's Corners, I saw the dark tents of the Enfield Firemen's Fair beneath the dark and unmoving Ferris wheel.

The state highway had just been widened and given a new coating of asphalt, the surface now so smooth that the truck seemed airborne, an illusion intensified as we rose and descended with the hills. The fragrance of newly cut clover and timothy, punctuated now and then with the different sweetness of freshly mowed lawns, accompanied us as we glided along. We were on the road we habitually took to get to our respective jobs, but everything was transformed by the hour (we had the road completely to ourselves, and every house was dark) and our mission. How strange it was, to be floating through the air like this in a pickup truck driven by a son, to be a white-haired professor kneeling next to an animal that might be dying, while one's wife for forty-five years knelt by the animal's other side, her hair blown back by the wind!

As we neared Ithaca, we passed the house where the Colombian couple had established their goat dairy. They were parents of sixteen children; their offspring had become doctors, nurses, nuns, and business people, and had scattered about the world, some in Europe, some in the Middle East, others in Central and South America and Canada as well as in the United States, but every ten years the family came together for a reunion. Cris, Jean, and I had been invited to the goat farm for one of these gatherings. A number of picnic tables had been placed under the limbs of a grand tree in their side yard—that rarity, a full-grown American chestnut that had withstood the blight—and the main dinner fare was a calf roasted on a spit. The couple's children were middle-aged, with children of their own, some of whom had babies. The three older generations sang Colombian songs, and songs of the various countries in which they lived, to the accompaniment of a Spanish guitar.

But soon after that reunion, the goat barn caught fire from a malfunction of the heater used for pasteurization; all of the goats died in the blaze. The couple sold the house and left America to introduce the techniques of goat husbandry to the natives of an island kingdom in the Persian Gulf. How brave and undeterred that elderly couple had been! I heard that the husband, Ignazio, died in a car accident in Mexico City while on a visit to a relative there. The new owners of the property had cut off the vast lower branches of the chestnut. Had those branches decayed, or did the new owners simply want grass to grow beneath the tree which had sheltered the picnic tables? As we drove by that house, I was aware of a kind of abyss or dark cavity, maybe in my mind or in the actual landscape, which once had contained the goat barn and the marvel of the chestnut as it had been.

Above us, through a gap in the clouds, I saw the Big Dipper, the end stars of the cup pointing toward the invisible North Star; indifferent as that glitter was to us and our journey, it shone down upon us as if we—Cris, the driver, and Jean and I, the silent kneelers—were figures in some allegory or mystery play that centered on a suffering Gandy but included everything that we journeyed by. In part, my response was an intensification of my feelings on the night that Cris and I, the newborn kid in a box on my lap, had made a similar journey, but now it was accompanied by something else.

The night air was tender not only with the pervasive smell of the various cut grasses, but with the ephemeral nature of our lives and all that we make, on this tiny planet: this was the theme of our play or allegorical tableau. It was a truth I may have long known but never had experienced so absolutely, in body and mind, as I did from the bed of Cris's pickup truck, looking at the seemingly empty structures (the passing houses and barns) that we humans build to provide, in addition to their utility, a necessary illusion of permanence and security. And yet what extraordinary effort we put into these delicate constructions—in creating them from our dreams, and after that in maintaining and prettifying them!

These feelings came, I suppose, not only because of the dark cavity I saw or imagined but because I was conscious of Jean's age as well as my own and was remembering a huge but broken slab of stone at the entrance of our house and was stroking a black sail that belonged both to an idealized animal from my own mythology and one that might now be dying. However much we humans may believe that we share an understanding with them, animals have shorter lives and can't speak; and maybe these are reasons that our experiences over the years with our animals can serve as a metaphor for much that remains more implied than said in our relationships with other humans during the longer curve of our own brief lives. From the crest of the hill, I saw the streetlights of Ithaca, and lights of the roads surrounding another dark cavity, one that held the deep waters of Cayuga Lake.

At the veterinary hospital, a light had been turned on for us at the emergency entrance of the small animal clinic, and two white-coated young women were waiting at the door. They carried the litter—Gandy was now completely passive—into an examining room. Cris left, to put his pickup truck in the nearby parking lot. Jean and I stood in the hallway. Though the quarters in the small animal clinic are cramped, preventing it from seeming the cathedral nave the large animal clinic had been to me when Cris and I brought the kid, it still was a comforting sanctuary. I was glad to be a teacher at a university whose faculty includes surgeons and other competent veterinary specialists who don't mind being waked at midnight or 3 A.M. to care for a newborn kid or a middle-aged dog of mixed breed.

In addition to gratitude, I was still feeling giddiness from the ride, and asked Jean if the trip had seemed strange to her. She said that she had never been so aware of the evanescence of life or the fragility of houses. We are separate people, Jean and I, and our personalities differ; but we have been married a long time, and sometimes our emotions coalesce like that. Because we are separate, I can't say what the road from our house to the veterinary hospital signified to her that night, but to me it was (and remains) the present section of a road I've been traveling a long time.

VIII. THE POND HOUSE

It is now mid-August of the following year. I have found no remedy—other than rock salt mixed with kitty litter in icy weather—for the broken slab at the front door. Jean and I, though, have done something about the pond. We've had it dredged, deepened, and doubled in area; we have put in a sand beach and built a dock for diving. Presently we are finishing the construction of a little pond house, to be used as a cabana and as a Scandinavian-like summer house in which one can be lulled to slumber on sultry nights by the sound of frogs, waking to watch the great blue heron that visits the pond while the morning mists are rising from it, and that returns each evening. The house will serve other good purposes, too: since it will have a wood stove, we can use it as a warming room for ice-skating parties, and as a complement to the sauna that Cris plans to purchase.

Jim, our youngest son, has done much of the heavy work during visits between his film jobs in New York and elsewhere; he cleared the space of underbrush, dug the post holes, decided to add a deck in front of the pair of sliding glass doors that face the pond, and helped install the roof and siding. To my mind, it's far more impressive than that quaint and precariously built summer house used as a major setting in the film *My Life As a Dog*. We are building it as carefully as we can, to outlast us all.

On weekends, Jean, Cris, and I have been working toward its completion; on weekday afternoons, Gandy accompanies me (I now teach only in the spring terms) for the several hours I usually spend on the structure, working on tasks I can handle by myself while others earn their salaries. Sometimes Gandy watches me, muzzle on her single front paw; sometimes she plays with two neighboring dogs, Butterscotch and Derby. Though Gandy hops like the rabbit she might have been chasing the night of her injury, she can run for short distances as fast on three legs as Butterscotch and Derby can on four. On weekends, when I and the other members of my family get overly hot from our labors, we go swimming; Gandy, half Labrador that she is, loves the water, and swims along with us. (I was alarmed when she first jumped in the pond, for I was afraid that the loss of a front leg might cause her to drown.) Like the rest of us, Gandy is as happy as she knows how to be.

1991

An
Ode for
St. Cecilia's Day

EVER SINCE my family moved to a classical revival farm-house in 1962, my study has been the old parlor, the frames of its windows and doors fluted to resemble Greek columns. Above my desk, positioned between two of the windows, is an untidy bulletin board. Amid the impaled but transitory memos are four mementos that have stayed put for years. One is a small reproduction of "The Polish Rider," which may or may not have been the work of Rembrandt, another is a copy of Paul Cadmus' charcoal sketch of E. M. Forster, and a third is a copy of a photograph of Anton Chekov. (Of all the writers who have influenced my life, Forster and Chekhov remain the most important.) The fourth is intended to be read, not looked at, and it is tacked to the very center of the board. It is a paragraph that I copied from Sylvia Townsend Warner's translation of Marcel Proust's essay "The Return to the Present," and this is what it says:

The fine things we shall write if we have talent enough, are within us, dimly, like the remembrance of a tune which charms us though we cannot recall its outline, or hum it, nor even sketch its metrical form, say if there are pauses in it, or runs of rapid notes. Those who are haunted by this confused remembrance of truths they have never known are the men who are gifted; but if they never go beyond saying that they can hear a ravishing tune, they convey nothing to others, they are without talent. Talent is like a kind of memory, which in the end enables them to call back this confused music, to hear it distinctly, to write it down, to reproduce it, to sing it. There comes a time in life when talent, like memory, fails, and the muscle in the mind which brings inward memories before one like memories of the outer world, loses its power. Sometimes, from lack of exercise or because of a too ready self-approval, this time of life extends over a whole lifetime; and no one, not your own self even, will ever know the tune that beset you with its intangible delightful rhythm.

I suppose I put that paragraph in the center because it connects talent in writing to music and memory, and because it communicates something about the spirituality that hovers, ghostlike, within the painting; that lies, as quest, within Forster's novels; and that—since it is, after all, unattainable, except in the most relative of terms—explains the paralysis of so many of Chekhov's characters, as well as the compassion that marks this most objective of writers. To Forster, "music is the deepest of the arts and deep within the arts," a view implicit in Proust, who seems to associate it with an even deeper memory.

Were we born, then, with a knowledge, however faint, of some ancient, truth-bearing tune? Pythagoras believed in the music of the spheres. Such a belief lingered on, long after Copernicus; as a conceit, it underlies the odes composed in late seventeenth-century London as part of the annual festival organized by the gentlemen of the Musical Society for the Feast of St. Cecilia, the patron saint of music, on November 22. According to the jacket of one of my most worn recordings, Henry Purcell's "Ode for St. Cecilia's Day," the members of the society "foregathered in the morning at St. Bride's Church, where a service was performed by the most skilled musicians, and a sermon was preached in defence of Cathedral Music, which had lately been suppressed under the Puritans." The members then "repaired to Stationers Hall to hear the new ode composed in Cecilia's honour, after which they sat down to a banquet." For the 1692 festivities, Purcell set to music a poem by Nicholas Brady, Chaplain to the Queen, which claims not only that music is "nature's voice, thro' all the wood and creatures understood, the universal tongue" but that it is the "soul of the world" which "inspired . . . the jarring seeds of matter . . . the scattered atoms," to bind together "in one perfect harmony."

Though I like that claim of kinship between music and nature, I've always preferred John Dryden's expressions of the conceit to Brady's. Dryden's "A Song for St. Cecilia's Day," the first and simpler of the two odes he wrote for the festivities, precedes Brady's by five years, and concludes with this Grand Chorus that connects the beginning of things with their ultimate dissolution:

As from the pow'r of sacred lays
The spheres began to move,
And sung the great Creator's praise

To all the blest above;
So, when the last and dreadful hour
This crumbling pageant shall devour,
The Trumpet shall be heard on high,
The dead shall live, the living die,
And Music shall untune the sky.

The meaning of Proust's paragraph is as elusive as that found in music, its values expressed by similes that have no original reference or source other than, perhaps, an implied origin of matter and thought; and the rhythms of his phrases, as captured in the translation, are those of music as well. Like Dryden's Grand Chorus, it moves from beginnings to endings; the progression is just as inevitable for the individual—for "us"—as it is for the celestial bodies. When I first came across the Proust passage more than thirty years ago, I suppose I thought of it as applicable only to writers, particularly those who—like Proust himself—depended upon the power of memory; but long before I used it as a modern-day equivalent of the talismans of my superstitious or reverent distant ancestors, tacking it to my bulletin board as if it were an emblem of a fish or beads of grain, I thought of it as applicable to the potentiality that existed not only in me but in every human being.

I've been meditating on such recondite matters ever since my wife and I returned from a winter vacation that included an overnight visit in Virginia with an old friend of ours we hadn't seen in decades. Our friend is a widower who lives with a handicapped son, and the story he told us—a parable about the power of music to invoke memory—became in my mind the theme of the final movement of a symphony of memory, preceded by musical themes long familiar. Events from my memory, in which music flows as a current, would recur in this new work as a kind of reprise.

* * *

According to my edition of *The Columbia Encyclopedia*, St. Cecilia was a "2d or 3d cent., Roman virgin martyr. She is remembered daily in the Mass. An ancient and famous account of her life is factually valueless. As patroness of music she is represented at the organ." All of the St. Cecilia Day odes that I have come across emphasize the organ to such an extent that it becomes not only her instrument but almost her being. ("When to her Organ vocal breath was giv'n," Dryden's first ode to St. Cecilia says, "An angel heard, and straight appear'd,/Mistaking earth for heav'n.") Organs made the grand sounds that my parents loved best, and those sounds were a major reason for their church-going and for the expensive radios that my father bought in my childhood. For my mother, organ melodies repre-sented, I am sure, a spiritual love beyond understanding, one that underlay her love for every member of her family; for my father they provided the spirituality he unsuccessfully, but unceasingly, sought to find in his material goals.

The closest approximation I could make to the sounds of the organ came from a Marine Band harmonica that I ordered by mail from the M. Hohner Co. It arrived in a blue plush case with instructions for playing a number of songs, and I learned to play them all, as well as many tunes of my own devising. Melodies, derivative as they may have been, seemed to originate without effort in my mind, as if they were variations of a melody I already knew something about, one full of wonder; and whenever my

parents visited friends or relatives who had pianos, I would pick
out my little tunes with the fingers of one hand.

When I was nine or ten, my father's restless pursuit of new
enterprise took the family south, to western Kentucky and then
to Arkansas. In Little Rock, I was given a pocket-sized pamphlet,
"The *Arkansas Democrat* Song Book," published by the afternoon newspaper. I still remember all of the songs, including the
one that begins, "Arkansas, Arkansas, I salute thee,/'Tis the place
I call home, sweet home." I sang so much in Arkansas that I
thought I had strained my voice, for I suddenly lost the ability to
sing on key. Perhaps it was a consequence of puberty. It happened, though, soon after my father left the family to live with a
woman in a distant state, and at the same time I also lost my
mathematical aptitude. Neither of these abilities ever returned
to me, though my father did return to my mother during my
senior year in high school.

During the years of his absence, my mother, my older brother,
Jack, and I lived for some months in a small second-floor apartment in Flint, Michigan, supported by Jack's pay as a work-study
student at General Motors Institute. We had no money to give
each other Christmas presents, but I did have a bicycle which I
sold for ten dollars, enough to buy a second-hand table radio, so
that the three of us—my mother, in particular—could listen to
organ and other holiday music. No purchase has ever given me
such pleasure. The radio was oval-shaped, and the grid supporting the gold speaker cloth reminded me of the trusses supporting
church ceilings. "Simplex" was its trade name, stamped on a little
metal plate. I still see my mother seated before it, her white hair
haloed by the dial light, listening to "He shall feed his flock," a
solo that I will always associate with the longing for an absent

family member. For me, such a longing was transfigured into a kind of metaphysical desire that had nothing to do with religious faith. (I think my response to that solo became part of my response, when I was much older, married and with three sons, to an aria sung by Sarastro in *The Magic Flute.* The words that he sings declare the achievement of love and brotherhood, but to my ears the melody belies this meaning, turning them into a profound wish, a yearning within the soul for the harmony that forever must elude it.)

* * *

In the Second World War, some soldiers carried little Bibles in the breast pocket over their hearts—Bibles bound in steel to bolster the protection of their faith. In place of the Bible, I carried a simple tune, one of the major themes of Brahms' "Symphony No. 1." My thirteen weeks of infantry basic training in Georgia are interminable even in recollection, for during those weeks I became a pariah. By acts of defiance so trivial I incorrectly thought they might escape notice, I resisted the constant attempts to reduce or negate my personality for the sake of absolute obedience to the military will. For twice wearing my helmet at a slight tilt at morning roll call, I was threatened with the stockade. Given my detestation of weapons, it is hardly surprising that I was the poorest marksman in my platoon. When I was given a bayonet to attach to my M-1, I thought I might vomit. Ordered by a drill sergeant to growl as I stabbed that bayonet into a gunny sack stuffed with straw, I could not, and so was threatened once again with the stockade. It was in keeping with military logic that, upon the completion of basic training, I was separated from the rest of my platoon; the rest were sent off to college to learn foreign languages and mathematics while I was shipped as a rifleman to an infantry division headed for combat in Europe.

My innocence was as stubborn as it was monumental. Only years later did I come to understand that I was a common enough paradox of that time, an innate pacifist caught up in a morally necessary war. Then, I knew only that the war never should have been allowed to happen. Believing that there was only one human race, I had written, shortly before my induction, an editorial for my college newspaper about our human brotherhood that stressed the universal language of music as typified by composers—Bach, Mozart, Beethoven, and Brahms—who were part of the culture of our enemy. In basic training, and later in France and Germany, that tune from Brahms' first symphony became my personal armor, my defense against sanctioned destruction and patriotic killing. A crucial part of the fourth movement, it is the slow and deliberate theme that is introduced by the violins, taken up by the woodwinds and then, in triumph, by the whole orchestra; toward the end of that final movement, the theme returns, a confirmation of its meaning. For me, it was an expression of my spiritual inviolability.

That it also had become something else—a statement of moral or spiritual supremacy—I realized one evening in France, as I was walking the main street of a village my division had recently occupied. A fellow American—a corporal like me, and one whose build was so similar to mine that he could have been my double—passed the other way, his helmet set at a rakish angle; he was whistling a more intricate tune than the one I carried in my mind. It was familiar to me; after he had vanished into the darkness, I puzzled over it, finally recognizing it as a theme from Brahms' *second* symphony, a work sometimes considered an advance over the first. This melody, in any event, lay beyond my powers to whistle or even to hear in its entirety in my head. I felt for that whistler no brotherhood at all; rather, I felt him to be an antagonist who had bested me in a competition.

* * *

After my discharge from the Army, I entered graduate school. In 1950, when I was appointed to my first full-time teaching post, as an assistant professor of English at Morehead, then a small state college in eastern Kentucky, I had not as yet written my doctoral dissertation. No period of my life is so intimately connected with music as the six years my family spent in that isolated valley in the forested hills of Kentucky. I suppose that the isolation, and a desire created in part from it, helped to make music so crucial to Jean and me. Except for WQXR, the radio station of the *New York Times,* the surrounding hills interfered with broadcast reception; because of some quirk caused by topography, WQXR reached our living room (but nowhere else in that little town, and here only after dark) with all the clarity and volume of a local station. Martin Bookspan, who each evening announced the selections of a long program of classical music, became a nightly presence, an incorporeal traveler from another realm whose ethereal passage had been paid for by a retailer of records named Sam Goody. During those mornings that Jean (who was the college's publicity department as well as its journalism teacher) and I worked at home, we listened to the latest release of the Musical Masterworks Society, a record subscription club we had joined.

Music even entered into the nightly baths I gave Larry, our older son, in his fourth and fifth years. We sat at opposite ends of the tub. I would hold his ankles, and swish him on his soapy bottom back and forth in rhythm to the traditional song for learning the ABC's—"A" bringing him toward me, "B" sending him back, with the swishing getting rapid enough to send suds to the floor in the sequence "LMNOP," which squeezes extra letters into the tune. Whenever we came to a letter in his first name, he would grin and hold up one hand, raising both for the repetition of the "R"; after he learned to do that with his first name, he learned to do with it the last name as well, and soon was the one singing all the letters of the alphabet as I swished him back and forth.

Three other department members, including the chairman, had been appointed around the same time that I was, and music as much as literature was the bond that made our separate families a single family. Our houses were only a short walking distance apart. Fran, the wife of the chairman, was a pianist who had a particular aptitude for teaching children how to play the instrument. Though she was anything but an indulgent teacher (several of her pupils won state and other competitions), children of all ages took lessons from Fran not on parental command but because they wanted to. Larry, for example, was only five on the morning he woke Jean and me at dawn, dressed in his suit and clip-on bowtie and carrying the briefcase I had used in graduate school. Apparently he had overheard a comment that Fran had made to Jean the previous day: observing Larry as he was hitting the keys of an old typewriter, Fran remarked, in surprise, that his fingers already were strong enough for the piano and that she might try a lesson with him early some morning, before her other pupils came. "Tie my shoes," Larry instructed Jean that dawn. "I'm going for my piano lesson." (Often, when he comes home to our upstate New York farmhouse for a visit, Larry, who is now in his early forties, sits down before the piano—a Steinway professional upright that we bought for him not long after that initial lesson.)

One of my new colleagues, Tom, was not only a specialist in Renaissance literature, but a musicologist and a violinist, and his wife, Sally, was a pianist. During the years they lived in Morehead, Tom worked on what was to become a three-volume study of the music in Shakespeare's plays; and he and Sally organized a small group of instrumentalists to play ancient music. To approximate the sounds of the harpsichord, they attached thumbtacks to the hammers of an old piano.

In addition to teaching speech and drama courses, P. C., another new member, directed, and sometimes acted in, the college plays; his wife, Linda, whom he had met while both were theater students at Chapel Hill, also performed in the productions, and helped the students to collect and sew the clothes they needed for their roles. Linda and P. C. bought a piano at the same time Jean and I did, for their daughter, like Larry, wanted to study with Fran. Linda, who had performed in musicals at Chapel Hill as well as in summer stock, liked to sing; and P. C., who as a child had himself studied piano, enjoyed playing hymns and other familiar songs.

Each member of our department taught five courses every term. Regardless of specialty, we each taught at least two courses in freshman composition, as well as a sophomore course in which writing was also emphasized. The paper-grading was so time-consuming that our social gatherings were often parties at which the week's compositions were passed out equally to teachers and their spouses. After we finished with our corrections, usually around midnight, we drank beer or wine (purchased illegally, since the county was dry) while listening to Bach or Mozart.

Early one June, I left for my graduate school to take the oral examination on my recently completed dissertation. Upon my return, Linda and P. C. accompanied Jean and me on an excursion to a nearby state park. Having passed my examination, I was, for the moment, relaxed, and my companions, who shared my happiness, were equally serene—even Linda, who suffered moments of nervous tension and was on medication for high blood pressure. We had left our children with others in our extended family—something we rarely did, but which probably abetted the harmony of that day. We rode horseback, swam in the lake, and cooked a meal over a barbecue pit. Driving home but not wanting the pleasure to end, I took a side road—hardly more than a pair of tracks—that led us over a hill and ultimately to a little church or chapel on the banks of what I later identified, from a map, as a stream called Grassy Fork. Wholly by chance, I had brought us at sunset to a place of enchantment. The church had the name of no denomination on it, but its immaculate condition indicated it was still in use, as did the neatly graveled parking lot on the opposite side of the stream. A much better road led to that parking lot. A small ferry or barge, connected to an overhead cable and no doubt propelled by poles, brought worshippers across the water. The door was unlocked. Inside were maybe six rows of pews, a lectern, and a piano with a stool. I don't believe any of us said anything. P. C. sat on the stool and immediately began to play the music that the hymnal on the piano rack was opened to. The rest of us stood by his side, singing that hymn—"I Walked in the Garden Alone"—and then other religious songs that all of us knew from childhood; he played, and we sang, until the room became too dark for any of us to see the music. Did I sing on key, as confident in my voice as were

Jean and Linda and P. C. in theirs? Maybe I did on this one occasion, for I sang without thinking I couldn't; I was nothing but a voice that merged in melody with other voices.

The images of the rutted and boulder-strewn road that brought us to that remote church by the stream as the sun was touching the opposite hill, of the exterior and interior of that church, and of the faces of the singers floating in the gathering dark—these images, carried along by song, hold all my memories of Morehead within them. All that day, though, we had been celebrating the acceptance of a dissertation that was the final requirement for the doctorate I needed for a position at a school with a less demanding teaching load; I was offered such a job at Cornell, and so, in the summer of 1956, Jean and I and our children left the hills of eastern Kentucky for those of the Finger Lakes region of upstate New York.

* * *

Soon after we left, all three of the families that had been so closely bound to ours also departed for other institutions in Florida, North Carolina, and Virginia. When, in the early 1970s, Tom was invited to Cornell to give a lecture on the music in Shakespeare's plays, he and Sally stayed with us. Except for this visit, the only contact Jean and I had with the others over the decades were Christmas cards expressing wishes for an eventual reunion sometime and somewhere, and messages of loss—Linda was the first to die, followed by Sally; and then, several years later, by Fran's husband, our old chairman, Hugh.

We learned of Linda's fatal stroke on the day of her burial. P. C. phoned us from Virginia that night, to tell us; Jean and I talked with him for half an hour or more. His gentle and tentative voice was just as I remembered it, and it recalled his tall but thin and slightly stooped frame—a body that may have reflected his modesty, but gave little indication of the staunchness and stubborn determination of his character. The first time I had met him, I had liked him at once; he had told me of his experiences as an actor, recounting some incidents that were funny and others that were harrowing, but had done so in such a shy or apologetic manner that I thought (until they were later confirmed by Linda and others) he might be improvising the stories for my entertainment. On this night, he spoke of Linda's two previous strokes, which had deprived her of speech, and of how he had given up his position as theater director of a Portsmouth college to help her learn to articulate again; and he also told us about their children. Linda had given birth to a boy shortly before Jean and I had left Morehead; a second daughter had been born to them in Portsmouth. The boy had been born with a defect that had stunted his physical and mental growth. Though it finally had been diagnosed, and an operation performed to correct it, his doctors had said that Ted would develop only slowly and probably not live many years. P. C., who had been tending to Linda and Ted at home, said that now he'd have more time for helping Ted, and that he was thankful that Linda, as she was dying, was at least, thank God, able to speak. After that phone call, our only contact with P. C. came from the Christmas notes. We learned of the college graduation of both daughters; of how the younger had gone to England for a job, and had married there, while the older was employed in Portsmouth as an administrative officer for a local bank. And we learned, too, that Ted, remaining at home under P. C.'s care, had defied the predictions of the doctors. Not only was he alive, he was as happy and as adjusted to his impairment as possible; indeed, he was well

enough that he and P. C. had flown to London for a vacation with
the younger daughter and her husband.

*   *   *

In January of the present year, with the Gulf War imminent, both
Jean and I became apprehensive and restless; all of my own old
abhorrence for humanity's long and banal recourse to military
might had returned. We decided to commune with the alligators,
egrets, and herons in the Everglades—and we decided to drive
to the southern tip of Florida in a leisurely manner, stopping off
at places we'd never been. We must have wanted, above all, to see
P. C., for we contacted him—to make sure he and Ted would
welcome a visit—before we made any other plans.

Though we found P. C.'s house—a brick bungalow on a corner lot in a quiet residential district of Portsmouth—without
difficulty, we thought, at first, that he and Ted weren't at home,
for nobody responded to the first ring and we could see or hear
no signs of life within. We rang the bell again. Some inner door
apparently was opened, for we heard several voices, raised maybe
in argumentation; none of them sounded like P. C.'s. I was
checking the address I'd written on a slip, to make sure we'd made
no mistake, when Ted, P. C. standing behind him, opened the
front door. Both of them were smiling. "I remember you," said
Ted, shaking my hand; but thirty-five years ago, when we had last
met, he had been an infant. Now he seemed a boy of twelve or
thirteen with a humped back. "He remembers you from some
old photographs," P. C. said gently before embracing Jean and
me. The four of us then stood without talking, trying to adjust
what we held in our minds to what we saw, waiting for the old
images to dissolve, like ghosts, into the present selves. It takes but
an instant for this to happen to friends who have been absent

from each other for years; after it does, the youthful image can't be recalled until a second physical separation turns both past and present into images that are apprehended simultaneously in a kind of double vision that, like a stereoscope, provides depth.

P. C. was not nearly so tall as I remembered him. The slight stoop had become a considerable one, as if in sympathy for his son's deformity; and the thinness of his frame—which had accentuated his height—was gone, though his face remained gaunt. I thought it strange that he led us beyond the large living room with its comfortable-looking couch and chairs as well as its piano to a much smaller room without windows. The voices I had heard came from the television in this room, tuned to a soap opera. The only other light came from a bridge lamp between a worn overstuffed chair (an opened book lay on its seat cushion) and a sofa.

Ted turned off the sound of the television and showed us the machine P. C. had bought him for the hooked rugs he made. The machine stood in a corner of the room, by a straight-back chair that faced the television. P. C. pointed to the intricately-patterned rug that covered much of the carpet on the floor. Ted, he remarked, had made that rug, as well as the antimacassars on the sofa arms. He had also made the hall runner and any number of throw rugs elsewhere in the house, and—since it took so long, even with the machine, to make rugs or wall-hangings and other holiday gifts for his relatives—Ted was already at work, P. C. said, on his presents for the following Christmas.

Jean and I both praised his work, for it was carefully done and the patterns handsome ones; we wondered that he didn't sell them, through some arts and crafts shop in Portsmouth. Such a suggestion alarmed P. C. more than it did Ted, who simply said he had fun making them while he watched the soap operas and his Dad read a book; P. C. said, "It just wouldn't be *right* to sell them." His every gesture indicated a protectiveness of his son. Probably he felt that the selling of the rugs would be an exploitative use of Ted's handicap.

Ted was engaging in his openness and vivacity. He still seemed to be a boy—but one who could combine the simple language of a child with such words as "proclivity" and "comprehension" and "convolutions" and who would intersperse his conversation with phrases like "What I really mean to say, Dad, is . . ." He could recite the intricate plots of half a dozen soap operas, laughing at the silliness of them. When I made a pun, he understood it at once, stomping his feet to express his delight—a response so enchanting to me that I made a half dozen more, something I normally can manage with such profusion only after drinking half a bottle of wine. He showed Jean and me his prized collection of picture postcards—most of them photographs of mountains or monuments—sent to him over the years by relatives and family friends on their vacations. Before passing each one to us, Ted would examine it himself, his eyes shining as if he were seeing it for the first time. I could understand now why P. C. had brought us into this dark and womblike space in the middle of his house—this and not the living room with its piano and conversational grouping of furniture was the center of the life he shared with Ted, and he wanted to include us in its intimacies.

That evening, Myra, the daughter we had known in Morehead—the one who, like Larry, had studied piano with Fran—joined the rest of us for dinner at a restaurant of the kind that serves Italian food and that, run by a family, welcomes all members of anybody else's family. P. C. said that he had often gone there with Linda and the children. Though he hadn't been back for several years, the proprietor and many of the old customers greeted him and Ted as old friends; and other diners, familiar with him through the plays he once had directed, came to our table. Another family entered the restaurant, the father and grown son wheeling a litter on which a young woman lay. Despite her illness or handicap, she waved and smiled to the customers and waiters who applauded her. It was a good restaurant, and I was glad P. C. had brought us to it. Ted was normally on a strict diet, but had permission from his doctor to forego it on occasions as special as this one. P. C. reminisced about our Morehead years, remembering in particular another special day—the one that ended with the singing in the magical church by the river.

Toward the end of our long conversation at the restaurant, I asked Myra if she remembered the night—Ted had not yet been born; she had been maybe five—that she had cried, simply because P. C. hadn't punished her. Linda had been called out of town because of some emergency; P. C., desperately trying to complete the blocking for his upcoming production, had ignored Myra's attempts all day to attract his attention through acts of increasing mischief. But after he had put her to bed, her loud sobbing did draw his attention at last; when he came into the bedroom to take her in his arms and ask her what was wrong, she had replied, "Daddy, I did one bad thing after another all day long and you didn't even spank me!" The Myra who was more than forty said that since Linda's first stroke, P. C. had given his complete attention to the needs of his family, and it was too bad he no longer had the opportunity to be distracted from them by the profession he also had loved. It pleased her to see his happiness on this night, for it seemed to her that in his devotion to Ted he was slowly retreating from the rest of the world. Myra visited them so frequently, in the evenings after work and on weekends, that she kept half her wardrobe at the house. She obviously worried about these two family members she loved so much— her seventy-year-old father and her thirty-five year old sibling who remained his young child.

Ted not only set the table for breakfast the next morning, but made toast and bacon and coffee for Jean and me; as recompense for his hearty meal the night before, he ate only a small bowl of his prescribed cereal. After breakfast, he left for the inner room, to work on a rug while watching television, and P. C. invited us to drink our second cups of coffee in the living room. It was here that he finally began to talk in detail about what had happened to him and his family in the years since we had been separated. He spoke of his and Linda's growing concern about Ted, and of the many fruitless consultations with the family doctor and an array of different specialists over an impairment only they, the parents, could notice at first. Until Ted began to limp and some- times fall, the problem was considered a psychological one. Had it been been properly diagnosed in time—a cyst at the top of the spine prevented drainage from the brain—Ted might have suffered no abnormalities.

Linda and P. C. had tended to Ted in the precarious months following his surgery. Now, years later, he not only had lived far beyond the prediction, but actually was beginning to mature physically: he was approaching puberty more than two decades late. P. C. believed that Linda's anxieties about Ted had contrib- uted to, if not caused, her first stroke. *Her* specialist predicted that she would never regain her ability to speak, but P. C., who had considerable knowledge of speech disabilities, thought oth- erwise. He gave up theater, that time-consuming passion, so that he could spend hours each day working with Linda. In order to support his family, he began to teach evening courses in composition at the local community college, two or three or more each session. . . .

"Wait a minute, P. C.," I said. "Those are just as time-consuming, they're the courses you used to hate for the hours they took." I interrupted him, I suppose, because his voice, in telling this story, was again taking on that shy or apologetic tone that I once had associated with fabrications. The narrative was so painful to hear that I wanted to discover some error in it.

These evening courses, he said, met only once a week, and all of the grading for them could be done at home, by Linda's bedside or wheelchair. Though she had no way to tell him so other than with a nod, he knew she desperately wanted to learn to speak again. Her energy was so limited that she needed to rest—time enough for him to grade three or four papers—between the exercises he was coaxing her to do. Those exercises were futile. Suddenly one day he remembered Linda's love of music, of singing in particular. He wheeled her to the piano—the one they had bought for Myra in Morehead. He hit a key. "A," he sang. She opened her mouth, but made no sound. He hit the key again and again, singing "A," for she clearly was trying to sing it; and finally she made a quavering sound.

Using the piano keys, he taught her to sing "A" through "G." How she learned the rest of the alphabet, I don't know; perhaps—as I had done, in the bathtub with Larry—P. C. turned to the "Alphabet Song." Patiently he taught her, still at the piano, to sing words, and finally short sentences. Meanwhile, she was trying to learn to walk as well. After some physical therapy sessions at a clinic, she was able, so long as P. C. supported her, to take a few steps, and finally to walk without his assistance. She was never able to communicate without the help of melody, though. Throughout their remaining years together, they spoke together wholly in song, using the tunes—many of them hymns—most familiar to her. ("Do you want some toast, dear Linda?" is what I imagined him singing, to which she sang back, "Why, yes, my darling man.")

At this point, I no longer could bear to listen to such a narrative being recounted so mildly, so humbly, by a voice I knew so well, and fled to the bathroom to wipe a cloth across my face and then to stare at the strange image—a cowardly lion with a disheveled white mane, or maybe just a sad-eyed clown—that I saw in the mirror.

Later that morning, as we continued our drive toward the Everglades, Jean told me, as matter-of-factly as she could, what I had missed. Linda would take short walks outside, but only if P. C. accompanied her or at least stayed in sight. They increased the length of these walks until it was clear to him that she had the strength to walk around the block by herself, something she was afraid to do. "You can walk around the block alone," he would sing to her, for he knew that she needed to feel more confident and independent. "No, I can't, I can't, I can't," she would sing back, in this familiar duet from the opera of their lives together.

One morning he accompanied her down the steps and to the sidewalk, singing to her that today, for his sake if not for her own, she had to walk around the block alone. "I can't," she sang. "You must," he rejoined. "I'll try," she sang, and he turned his back on her to reenter the house before she could change her mind. Hidden behind the drapery of their living-room window, he watched as she looked toward the closed door before slowly moving along the sidewalk. She turned the corner by their house, and was lost to his view.

P. C. told Jean that the next half hour was the longest of his life. For the last fifteen minutes of it, he waited outside, pacing back and forth on the lawn. Thinking that she either had fallen or somehow had become lost, he was about to search for her in the car when he saw the small figure that just had turned the distant corner of their block and was walking with such studied deliberation toward him that, like an image in a dream, she seemed to be making no progress at all. P. C. is, as I have said, a stubborn person, and so he didn't rush to her. He remained at precisely the point on the sidewalk at which she had begun her journey, but his arms were upraised in victory as he sang down that long block to her, "You're going to make it, I knew you could." When her weaker voice became audible, she was singing, "Yes, I can, yes, I can;" and they were both still singing as they embraced.

After she had finished this story, I asked Jean if P. C. had named the melody that he and Linda were singing at its triumphant conclusion. "No," she said. "I think it should have been from 'The Ode to Joy,' though." "Let's imagine it was, then," I said.

"All right," Jean said, and began humming its grand tune. I joined in as best I could in my off-key way. We kept our eyes straight ahead, not looking at each other, though she reached for my hand and held it as we drove down the coastal highway.

*   *   *

Returning home from the Everglades, we listened on the car radio to news of the Gulf War from nearly the moment of the initial announcement; and, on television screens in various motel rooms, saw the permitted film clips of bomb hits and the like. Whether that brief war was truly a victorious one, I cannot say; the many parades this Fourth of July suggest that it was, despite

its aftermath of suffering and death to innocent people, and
maybe it assures the oil for more pleasure trips of the kind we
took. Such a victory—as well as many others of the sort that are
made into novels and films—means far less to me than the one
gained by Linda and P. C. If the story of their final years together
were made into a film, it would end, of course, with the embrace,
and "The Ode to Joy" would resound as the credits rolled.

Victories like that rarely conclude actual lives, though. Ahead
of Linda were the two strokes yet to come, as well as the second
series of singing lessons under her obstinate husband's resumed
instruction. Dying, she could say—*sing*—her name and a few
phrases, an accomplishment, as I have reported, that is a solace
to her husband, who lives on, with their handicapped son. A
longtime acquaintance of mine at Cornell, who now is an emeritus professor of classics, tells me that Herodotus records a remark
of Solon to Croesus to the effect that a man's life can be called
fortunate (*eutuches*) before he dies but can only be regarded as
truly prosperous (*olbios*) when it has been completed. "Look
upon that last day always," the grimmer Sophocles has his chorus
say in the concluding passage of "Oedipus the King." "Count no
mortal happy till/he has passed the final limit of his life secure
from pain." Still, it does seem to me that certain victories can be
significant enough to inform the rest of our lives with their
meanings, whatever the final outcome—an informing that, even
if it is lost to us at the very end, is available to those who survive
as chorus.

* * *

It was Linda and P. C.'s victory that made me want to compose
a celebration of music that would demonstrate the changing as
well as the constant nature of its influence upon me and others

as we slip through life together. That music stirs our memories is of course a commonplace; the smell of autumn leaves, or of wood smoke, is much the same kind of agent. No aroma, though, could have accomplished what music did for Linda, enabling a damaged brain to recover a lost function—to remember how to form words. In Linda's case, this power of music was summoned up by a shared spiritual desire, but music and the memory entwined with it can be used for less noble aspirations—for instance, to assert one's superiority to others, as was the case with me when I was a young soldier. Indeed, music has been used for some pretty dreadful human ends, such as the appropriation of certain Wagnerian themes to invoke a feeling of racial superiority. Under stress or disease, memory, abetted by music, can forego its search for a pure harmony that always must elude it, accepting a perceived part in preference to the unseen whole.

But what lies beneath or beyond the dimly remembered tune, "this confused remembrance of truths" we have never known, that Proust was reaching for? From the years of my concern with memory as the greatest invisible ally we have, I can offer only a hypothesis, though it is one supported by my readings of Forster and Chekhov as well as by my inner experiences. That hypothesis seems so valid to me that I have been modifying and expanding it for years. Each of us was born from the Earth to which we will return, and for the brief arc of individual existence we are separated from a universe so terrifying and incomprehensible to our conscious minds that we continuously are analyzing, and discriminating among, its parts, to make what sense we can of it and ourselves. Memory is the faculty that carries us as close to our origin in nature as we can get; in our unconscious minds it is ever at work, binding as best it can all that our consciousness must isolate. What it seeks, it never can have; with its unattainable desire for union—for freedom—memory is, I believe, the human soul. It is no wonder, then, that we speak in metaphor to approach truth, and find in music, whose rhythms may have affinities with the natural cycles, the elusive secrets that lie beyond even the words and images we create in the vain attempt to capture a harmony wholly indifferent to our strivings for it.

I began my exploration of memory over thirty years ago, as a search for personal meaning in a human and natural world whose sacredness had become apparent to me through my fear that we might soon annihilate not only ourselves but the robins and their nests. Fortunately, such an end has become less likely in recent years, though the quest for harmony remains un-fulfilled. I now am drawing my exploration to a close, while I—like civilization itself—am still in luck. I no longer listen to music as frequently as this celebration might suggest, and only in memory can recapture its emotional intensity. At seventy, though, I still put my trust in the music of the spheres, in a melody that from childhood on I could faintly hear, as if it were the dim remembrance of some ancient natural song; and from which (out of personal need, out of hope too that it would be in harmony with that of others) I have constructed this long tune of my own.

JAMES McCONKEY

has written novels, stories, and criticism
in addition to autobiography. Born in Ohio, he has lived
for more than thirty years in a farmhouse in the Finger Lakes
countryside. He is Goldwin Smith Professor of English
Literature, emeritus, at Cornell University, where
he currently is Advisor on the Arts
to the Provost.

STORIES FROM MY LIFE WITH
THE OTHER ANIMALS

has been set by The Typeworks in Minion, an excellent example of how far digital typesetting has progressed in the past decade. Designed by Robert Slimbach of Adobe Systems, Minion is a modern interpretation of a classic Renaissance "old style" face. All the faces in this family have their origin in the humanistic script developed and widely used in the late fifteenth and early sixteenth centuries. Scholarly publishers such as Aldus and Jenson converted the calligraphy of contemporary scribes into readable, elegant book faces, incorporating lively italics, ligatures, and "small capitals" as integral parts of the fonts.

Slimbach's design is especially suited for the demands of modern offset printing. It is even in color, calligraphic in spirit, and contains (*deo gratias*) a full range of italics, old style figures, ligatures, and genuine small caps, necessary appurtenances not often available in modern "recuttings." A successful synthesis of both historical precedence and contemporary design, Minion is perfectly suited for book work demanding a classic face designed for digital setting.

Designed by Vic Marks
Printed by and bound by
Haddon Craftsmen,
Scranton, Pennsylvania.